SONS COME AND GO,
MOTHERS HANG IN FOREVER

BOOKS BY WILLIAM SAROYAN

Novels

The Human Comedy
The Adventures of
  Wesley Jackson
The Twin Adventures
  (The Adventures of
  William Saroyan Writing
  The Adventures of
  Wesley Jackson, and
  The Adventures of
  Wesley Jackson.)
Tracy's Tiger
Rock Wagram
The Laughing Matter
Mama I Love You
Papa You're Crazy
Boys and Girls Together

Stories

Dear Baby
My Name Is Aram
Saroyan's Fables
Peace, It's Wonderful
The Trouble with Tigers
Love, Here Is My Heart
Little Children
Three Times Three
Inhale and Exhale
The Daring Young Man
  on the Flying Trapeze
The Saroyan Special
The Whole Voyald
The Saroyan Reader
I Used to Believe I Had
  Forever, Now I'm
  Not So Sure

Letters from 74 Rue Taitbout,
  or Don't Go But
  If You Must Say Hello
  to Everybody

Memoirs

The Bicycle Rider in
  Beverly Hills
Here Comes, There Goes
  You Know Who
Not Dying
Days of Life and Death
  and Escape to the Moon
Places Where I've Done Time
Sons Come and Go,
  Mothers Hang In Forever

Plays

The Time of Your Life
My Heart's in the Highlands
Love's Old Sweet Song
The Beautiful People
Sweeney in the Trees
Across the Board on
  Tomorrow Morning
Razzle-Dazzle
Sam Ego's House
A Decent Birth,
  A Happy Funeral
Don't Go Away Mad
Get Away Old Man
Jim Dandy
  (Fat Man in a Famine)
The Cave Dwellers
The Dogs, or
  The Paris Comedy, and
  Two Other Plays

SONS
COME AND GO,
MOTHERS
HANG IN FOREVER

William Saroyan

McGraw-Hill Book Company

NEW YORK   ST. LOUIS   SAN FRANCISCO

Book design by Ingrid Beckman.
Copyright © 1976 by William Saroyan.
All rights reserved.
Printed in the United States of America.
No part of this publication may
be reproduced, stored in a retrieval
system, or transmitted,
in any form or by any means,
electronic, mechanical, photocopying,
recording or otherwise, without the prior written
permission of the publisher.

An exclusive limited edition has been separately published.

3 4 5 6 7 8 9   FGFG   7 9 8 7 6

Library of Congress Cataloging in Publication Data

Saroyan, William, 1908
    Sons come and go: mothers hang in forever.

    1. Saroyan, William, 1908   —Biography.
I. Title.
PS3537.A826Z543   818'.5'209 [B]   75-43520
ISBN 0-07-054748-3

For Armenak
Takoohi
Hrupsimeh
Lucintak
Ahlkhatoon
Petros
Minas
Barunak
Garabet
Dikran
Aram
Hovakim
Levon
Missak
Mihran
Pepron
Strawsy
Cremo

Saroyans one and all

CONTENTS

[7]

[9]

SONS COME AND GO, MOTHERS HANG IN FOREVER

What It's All About

To BEGIN WITH, I not only believe I am William Saroyan, I believe it means something that I am. And then I believe that this meaning is large, and goes far, and is not ever going to be forgotten by the world and by the human family.

This is of course pure and pathetic vanity, and it comes straight from the Ideal Man of the Western World.

Jesus insisted that he was God, and the son of God. He also insisted that he was the whole human race, and the father of it, and the son of it, and the salvation of it, and the meaning of it, and love.

But he never said anything about absurdity, and he never indicated for one flash of time that he was aware of the preposterousness of his theory about himself. And he didn't even *try* to make the theory understandable in terms of the reality and experience of the rest of us.

For if everybody else is also not what Jesus said he was, what good is what he said?

In thinking of the brightest and greatest people I have ever met, I am unable to consider any of them free of this vanity, and a kind of raging *selfness* that almost equals evil.

Is the idiot, then, the good man?

Yes, the idiot is indeed the good man, but only because he doesn't know any better.

Still, it is always possible to believe that a reasonable goodness *can* appear in a human being, and therefore in the race itself, as a consequence of his both knowing a great deal and having experienced a great deal.

The person who is integrated from never having known disintegration, honest from never having needed not to be, virtuous from never having been tempted, is neutral, and slightly less than human.

There is no easy way for us to make sense of our historic success in putting up with ourselves, our foolishness, our fraudulence, and finally our innocence.

We are not perfectable, we just happen to have been complicated by the strange theory that we can become perfect.

Who are the great people that I met? George Bernard Shaw? Jean Sibelius? Diego Rivera? H. L. Mencken?

Well, the answer is yes, these are a few of the people, but they won't do, they are far too far off center. The people I am really thinking about are my father, my mother, their fathers and mothers, and my son, and my daughter, and all the rest of the closest of kin of all of these people.

And finally I am thinking of myself, how could I possibly not be, for I am *doing* this, which is also an act of vanity.

Is identity itself, then, a fraudulence?

Has identity the vulnerability and the flaw of pose, pride, arrogance, greed, all to the edge, even, of the committing of crime upon others?

Yes, I think both inherited and acquired identity in its very nature is helplessly fraudulent, but there we are, aren't we? We lose if we win, we lose if we lose, we lose if we tie, we lose if we don't play the game, we lose if we refuse to bother, we lose if we do nothing other than bother from the minute choice presents itself to us as a reality to the minute when choice also is irrelevant, impossible, and at least *questionable* as a means to a worthwhile end.

Life gives us choices that make fools of us, death gives us no choice at all, and yet we are expected to die as if we had planned it that way all along.

Thus, I can't be too surprised by the fool I have been, but *what* a fool I was, and year by year how it amazed my young mother, and how it must have astonished my dead father. He must have died a thousand new deaths as I moved up to the thirty-six years of his life, and then on and on, to thirty-two more years of my own. Well, what do we know? I *thought* I was right every time, but God knows what he thought, or how wrong I was, or how stupidly I was neither, but was only there.

A for Arlen for Armenia

IT ISN'T BECAUSE his name begins with the letter A that I
remember Michael Arlen first, it is something else again
entirely.

Several things again entirely. The most important thing
is that he was an Armenian. And he had written a book
that had been published when I was a telegraph messenger
in Fresno and had just bought my own typewriter and was
just beginning my own career as a writer.

The name of the book was *The Green Hat*, and the
name of the writer was Dikran Kouyoumdjian, which he
had changed to Michael Arlen.

His friends, however, including D. H. Lawrence, addressed him as Dikran. That is, they addressed themselves
to his reality rather than to his art, or to his invention of
himself.

Now, of course any sensible man has no choice but to
invent himself, or at any rate to add invention to what is
already there, and this fellow, who was just under thirty,
had added a lot to what he had been born with, and what
he had added I liked a lot.

He had been born with a perfectly designed head and
face, with a touch of mocking aloofness in the cynical
wisdom of the eyes. He was dapper, and he said dapper
things in dapper English. He had been born with a good,

tight, slim little body, and he had placed upon it the best clothes Saville Row could provide.

When I heard about him I was delighted. I knew there were Armenian writers who had written their poems, stories, novels, plays, essays, and histories in the Armenian language, men with such pen names as Raffi, for instance, or Narek, or such actual names as Khatchadour Abovian or Vahan Totoventz, but I hadn't heard of an Armenian who had written anything of any consequence in the English language, whatever his name might be, and I wasn't sure I was satisfied with my own—that is, Saroyan.

How about Sahara, instead?

Wouldn't that be harsh, dry, hard, desolate, windblown, and a killer of all but the very hardy, brave, lucky, or experienced?

I said to myself when I heard about Michael Arlen, If he can do it, I can do it. He's an Armenian and I'm an Armenian. He comes from Manchester, and he went to London. I come from Fresno, and I'm going to New York. He comes from middle-class business people. I come from no-class poetry people—at least on my father's side, dead since 1911, poor fellow, never had a chance.

As for my mother's side, that's another story—they are something else, and thank God that they are, suppose both sides had been peachy and poetic, my goose would have been cooked at the outset.

Michael Arlen was a dandy, and we finally met when his fame had long since ebbed, and mine was still rolling up on the beach with the high tide. We spoke in Armenian, and instantly accepted one another, as different as we were.

In 1935 when Ernest Hemingway attacked me in that ever-fat magazine, *Esquire*, because in one of my earliest stories I had kidded him about his fascination with bull-fights, I wrote directly to him instead of replying in the pages of the magazine, for money, and free publicity for everybody. Hemingway wrote back and tried to justify his petty remark about Michael Arlen: "Don't forget there was another Armenian writer, and you know what happened to him." His attempt to justify his petulance did not succeed. As far as I was concerned, Ernest Hemingway was ever after a very literary (and sensitive) soul, not a fearless hero of the physical world.

Michael Arlen may very well have been only every other inch a gentleman, as Rebecca West is said to have put it, but few men are *that* much.

In 1945 at the Pierre Hotel bar, at our first meeting, he said that he loathed his writing, but that he was going to write one true book, his own story, to be called *The Humble Peacock.*

Did he write it?

Did he even *begin* to write it?

I don't know.

Arlen.

Armen.

Armenian.

Michael Armenian.

Armenak and Takoohi

AND THEN THERE IS the matter of kith and kin, kitch and
koo, the females kitching at the tiny males and everybody
kooing at them and talking crazy in three or four languages,
Armenian, Turkish, Kourdish, and some kind of English,
what is a man to do trying his best to figure out what the
real nature of his exile is and from whence, for isn't he
indeed among his own kith and kin?

Deepest of all and most difficult of all to speak about with
anything like meaning *is* this matter of kith and kin, the
actual living breathing kith and kin each of us has, and
must put up with.

Who is that hairy bastard with his enormous genitals
hanging down, and his big sex smell and breath and voice
and body and face? His big cock and balls beneath all that
stupid hair, he looks like hell, what's *he* doing here, too?
Haven't we had enough of him cluttering up the fucking
place, get the bastard out of here with his big importance
and large language and his rotten despair and rage and
his terrible politeness and sighs and wishing he were
dead, well let him have his wish and be dead and begone,
this is no place for old cock and balls and hair and sweat
and piss and fart, oh he thinks nobody knows he sneaked
out the fart, but it was him, he is the only one whose farts
have that smell, big and all-tragic and lonely and desperate,

let him go, we've had enough of him around here, haven't we, you and me, Mama, you with your big bosom all laden with the scent of milk and Woolworth talcum powder and perfume out of a dime bottle labeled Wild Rose, and your soft full white arms and your different face and long black hair and the sweetest sweat that ever came from a living creature and a fart altogether nicer than that old tragic fellow's fart with his long sighs of longing for God knows what, Mama, Mama, it is you and me, isn't it, it isn't you and anybody else, is it, especially not you and him, is it, get him out of here, he's insensitive, his huge hanging equipment tells us that instantly, doesn't it, Mama, he did his work, he did his duty, what's he want now, Mama, does he want to grab you and do his work some more, well, Mama, shame on you if you let him, shame on you if you want him to, for I am here, and if I am not the one, then what in God's name am I doing here, why was I brought here?

Now, my father, Armenak of Bitlis, as I think of him, the failed poet, the failed Presbyterian preacher, the failed American, the failed theological student, up and died in a way that was clearly damned foolish and deeply discourteous, and yet in another way a great kindness to me, since it put me into very real exile before I was three, and permitted me not to find my father a monster with a monstrous purpose, to do to my girl, my mother, the things that I was put into this life and world to do to her, without my knowledge of course but settled in my bones and nerves and mind and memory and sleep and all of the known senses and all of the unknown equivalent of senses and all of the unknown elements of human reality that nobody had yet so much as suspected as being there at all, died of a ruptured appendix one day, in the heat of a grand July afternoon, in 1911, just asked for lots of water with which to try at least, to *try*, to quench his terrible thirst, the last thirst of life, and his wife, the mother, the woman, the girl, the first sexual party of my experience, letting me out of herself by that much enlarged channel into which she had not so long ago let him in, old Armenak, melancholy, in despair, died at the age of thirty-six, alive in Bitlis in 1874, dead in San Jose in 1911, and there she was with two daughters and two sons, my own kith and kin all of them, and I don't remember my father at all, never saw him by accident in his nakedness, with his great genitals dangling at the same place of the body where the woman's door is.

And so I could love and admire my father and did love and admire him, and at the same time refused to believe in his death, and permitted myself to believe that he would come back, somehow come back to me—the hell with the others, the rest of the kith and kin, my father would come back to me, for I had never known him at all, and they had, and I loved and admired him most, for to me he was a perfect man and had no cock and balls and didn't fart or anything else gross and stupid and real and shitty like that, at all.

An Orphanage Far Far Away

If I were to start at the top, as the saying is, remembering the people of the world I have met, one of the very first would have to be John Wesley Hagen, the Superintendent of the Fred Finch Orphanage in Oakland.

I met him in August of 1911, soon after Takoohi Saroyan had taken me to that place, and then in accordance with staff instructions had taken me to a small room in which to negotiate the separation.

I began to cry and she said, "No, you are a man now, and men do not cry." So I stopped crying.

She gave me a mechanical toy which was named *The Coon Jigger*. Wind him up and he danced, himself all tin, dancing madly on a tin stage. Once was enough, though.

I was then alone in the small room that I still remember as having smelled deathly as well as oily from some kind of stupid furniture polish, for what could possibly be more stupid to a small boy under such circumstances than the polishing of dismal institutional furniture?

After I had been alone long enough to go over my whole future life, perhaps several times, after surely not more than three or four very quiet minutes, the door from the main office opened and in came this man who seemed very big and very old.

The man was Mr. Hagen, as he was called, and he was surely not more than six feet tall, not heavy at all, and not more than forty years of age.

"Well, now," he said, "let's go right on being sensible this way."

Thus, I arrived officially into a world I had never imagined existed at all, let alone a world that I would somehow manage to inhabit for five years. I used to believe it had been four years, but it turned out that I was there along with my brother Henry and two sisters Cosette and Zabel from 1911 to 1916. I had always mistakenly believed that I had left in the summer of 1915.

From that year, 1915, there are a number of names that come back to me. Art Smith, a trick airplane aviator at the San Francisco Fair, officially called the Panama-Pacific International Exhibition. Beachey, also a trick loop-the-loop aviator, whose full name escapes me. And Dario Resta, who raced automobiles. Now, the thing to notice about these names is that they belong to daredevils, and that in my early boyhood I admired these men and the things they did.

On the other hand, there was a man with a beard who lived about four hundred yards above the orphanage, in the Oakland hills, whose name was Joaquin Miller, and although I never met him, either, I admired him, too, even though I knew he was not a daredevil, he wrote poems.

They were the big names: three daredevils and one poet.

My brother Henry in a group of eleven or twelve older boys did in fact, with Mr. Hagan or his wife Lillian Pender, go up one afternoon by appointment to call on Joaquin Miller, and Henry actually saw him.

I wished then that I had been along, and I still do. That would have been just right for me. Only three or four years old and already in the presence of a writer of poems. Henry said that Joaquin Miller had a big white beard, so I connected him instantly to the drawings of God in Sunday School books.

John Forderer was one of the members of the orphanage board of directors, and on several occasions I saw him with his fine red hair and beard. He used to take the kids for a ride in one of the earliest automobiles of Oakland, but one day the car was struck by a slow-moving locomotive, and a very small boy from my Ward was instantly killed, along with John Forderer himself. The seven or eight other kids in the car were only badly shaken up.

The Irish cook, whose specialty was meat pie, was hearty and loving, but I don't remember her name. Did I ever know it? I believe not, for how would I have ever forgotten the name of such a beautiful large woman?

Blanche Fulton was a volunteer social worker who took all of the boys in our Ward on various little outings and excursions, bought paper and Crayolas for us at her own expense, and expressed delight in our work, or disappointment when we behaved without sensitivity and courtesy. I used to whistle a lot, for instance, and for some reason she was always asking me not to—that is the worst thing I can say of her.

Miss Winchester was the big woman who for a while was the Matron of our Ward. Every Saturday morning we were obliged to trot to her, kneeling at the big bathtub, so that she could pick us up one at a time and dunk us into the water and scrub us, a procedure I hated and considered an outrage. I didn't need *her* to bathe me.

But you put up with the rules when your bulk weight is under forty pounds.

The Holy Family
of the Oakland Hills

ANOTHER CHARACTER of the early world was the youngest of the Ryan boys. The Ryans had a long rabbit hutch in their big garden in the hills above the Fred Finch Orphanage, and in the hutch were dozens of mysterious rabbits with watching eyes above quivering mouths. Even though I have forgotten the boy's first name, I haven't forgotten *him*, because what he had was ease, and that was a thing a man had to notice, if he was a man of the orphanage, because our boys *didn't* have ease.

They didn't like being where they were, and that dislike deprived them of ease. I especially didn't like being there. I believe that I hated that place more than anybody else who was there.

At any rate, I was the youngest to ever run away, aged five, into Oakland, where I meandered at will, unhindered, for who can say that a wandering boy's big brother, big sister, mother, or father, is not nearby, or that he does not live at a place just around the corner?

After dusk, however, I was found and taken back. I did not discourage the theory that I had been lost, for I liked the *word*, I liked the notion of it, and I even then suspected that it fairly accurately described my situation.

I *was* lost, I was not home, and I did not feel at ease.

I saw this lordly feeling flawlessly demonstrated in the

body, face, and style of this youngest of the Ryan boys: he *was* home, and he was at ease.

Well, they had this rather glorious mother, you see, who couldn't have been forty, with sons from eighteen down to my friend, aged seven or eight. We had met either at Sequoia School where I had just lately started, or while some orphanage boys were on a hike in the Oakland hills, looking for hazelnuts, waterdogs, lizards, snakes, or baby birds to take home and make pets of, for the idea of having a pet appeals to anybody in a penitentiary or an orphanage. And so, one day I traded a broken dollar-Ingersoll-watch for a baby owl and was considered a fool, but only by people over the age of fourteen. The poor little creature was dead the day after I made the trade, but I didn't care that the trade had been a poor one, I was only sorry my dear little feathered friend had died, that's all. For I had imagined us legendary in friendship, I saving the tiny creature from some kind of savagery, being eaten perhaps by hungry people from Sacramento, and the bird swooping down to pluck at the eyes of somebody trying to kidnap me to Borneo, possibly the Wild Man of that place himself—and the world stopping to notice with astonishment (and a nice lesson learned) the devotion of these two to one another—the great man as a small boy and the small owl grown to eagle-like maturity and increasing devotion to, if not utter admiration for, William Saroyan, and if you don't know who he is, or who he is going to be, you haven't lived.

Young Ryan one day somewhere along the line fell in with me as we trooped along Peralta Avenue and he said, "Come on over to the house and my mother'll fix us a sandwich."

I looked at him and saw how easy he was in expression, how open and casual, and this made me begin to wonder about some other people I had met. For the truth is that in

Luna Park (the name goes right on enchanting and haunting my sleep) I had met boys who were *not* from an orphanage, who were from families, but were indeed more orphan than any of us at Fred Finch Orphanage.

So here now was Young Ryan, and he was not in any way whatsoever an orphan. When he threw out casually the remark that his mother would make us a sandwich—*before* suppertime?—I was amazed, delighted, grateful, and full of curiosity about the woman herself.

She was indeed a woman, but like a girl, and just as open and casual as her youngest son, and any of the others, all of whom I had seen in action with older boys of the orphanage from time to time—flying kites, riding the tops of eucalyptus saplings, making the trees bend almost to the ground, in foot races, in bicycle races, in whittling stuff out of tree twigs, slingshots, and pointed sticks for rattlesnakes (even though our snakes were harmless and in fact quite beautiful, although it was our custom upon capturing one to snap its neck, like cracking a whip).

The sandwich she quickly made and handed to me tasted like truth itself, ham on a bun, with mayonnaise, lettuce, and mustard.

They *were* a family.

And I wanted *my* family.

But we were *never* like that. We were more crazy, angry, sad, caught up, fighting, involved.

The Rejected Mothers, Lillian Pender and Blanche Fulton

LILLIAN PENDER married John Wesley Hagen because the man she really loved wouldn't put up with her high-tone ways, or was killed in a train accident, or didn't really have a mind to marry anybody, but whatever the reason may have been, there was supposed to have been somebody else, somebody better, but she had finally accepted this rather plain Scot, because she wasn't getting any younger.

There was a touch of icy elegance to the lady, an aloofness, a kind of hauteur, although she probably was not a cold person at all.

But she didn't need to be warm as far as I was concerned. The warmth that came from Blanche Fulton, the volunteer social worker, who was indeed from a wealthy family, was also not thrown about in a way likely to annoy a small boy. Blanche Fulton was equal only to a deeply sincere and musical voice in expressing disappointment, for instance, in my failure to remember not to hum, whistle, or sing as I made line drawings with pencils and colorful pictures with crayons.

Blanche Fulton certainly didn't hate us. She cared about us enough to want to take us on trips to Luna Park, and it was she who took us one whole day to the San Francisco International Exposition, on a streetcar all the way to where the ferry was boarded, across the big bay, *Sailing, sailing, over Niagara Falls,* Teddy Dolan, Sammy Isaacs, and I sang as the little tub pushed its way steadily from Oakland to San Francisco, *Captain Dick lost his prick, and the fish ran away with his balls.*

But neither Lillian Pender nor Blanche Fulton were actually anything at all like real people to us—they were part of the orphanage, they came with the place, like the rooms and the furniture, the rules and the conspiracy among the inmates to get away some day and get even.

Get even for *what?* For the insult of being made a member of a kind of children's army, I suppose.

It was only after having finally left the place that I, for one, began to see the orphanage as not having been anywhere near as rotten as it might have been, and it was quite simply true that the Irish cook's meat pie was one of the finest table experiences of my young life.

Lillian Pender painted in oils, and she liked to try for portraits. Her portrait of the small boy who had been killed in the automobile accident was reproduced on a postcard. Everybody was encouraged to take forty or fifty of the cards and sell them to householders for whatever they cared to give—to pay for a stone for the little boy's grave.

Nobody turned me down, although only a few were lavish in the coins they put into my hand. I blew a dime on jawbreakers, and turned in about eight dollars.

Lillian Pender had me sit three times a week for three weeks, and then threw up her hands in despair. She couldn't paint my portrait. I just wasn't still enough or the same enough from day to day to be painted.

Bet your life I wasn't.

What names, what faces, what hands, what costumes they wore, what scents came from them, what voices they had, and how deeply useless and even outrageous their connection was with us, total strangers to them long after we had been there for years: for the simple reason that they were not ours, they were theirs, and there could not be any way to change that.

But they were fine women just the same. They tried their best to be mothers to the sons of unknown mothers, mad mothers, criminal mothers, and all kinds of other mothers. But the sons wouldn't have them, couldn't have them, had to have the original or no mother at all.

Eddie Emerian, the Pride of L Street

EDDIE EMERIAN LIVED four houses down on L Street just
around the corner from the house I lived in on San Benito
Avenue, number 2226. His people had come over to
America, and then all the way out from Ellis Island and
New York to the other end of the continent, to California,
and to Fresno, from the highland city of Bitlis, the city of
the Saroyans. But that isn't the only reason Eddie Emerian
and I were friends.

There is no explaining why out of three dozen boys in a
neighborhood one becomes a friend and the others are forever only acquaintances, or rivals, and even enemies.

Rivals for what? For excellence, of course, and in his
own chosen field Eddie was supreme—wrestling, usually
on the lawn of Emerson School, sometimes with D. D. Davis
refereeing. Nobody could give Eddie a real contest, except
me once in a while, and there was even a match in which
I put him down, but the Principal of Emerson School
didn't tap me on the shoulder and declare me the winner,
as I had thought he would and so had relaxed a little,
whereupon Eddie flipped like a great fish and had me up
and around and down, and D. D. Davis instantly tapped
him on the shoulder, so that Eddie was declared the winner
of that match, too. He did agree in private, though, that

I had actually won it, and that made me respect him more than ever.

Eddie Emerian did artful and amazing things, which might have been understood to be on behalf of wit, had there been anybody around to know about such a thing.

He certainly told me that he would take a brand-new Kissel Kar, for instance, because he loved the name of the thing, and the style of it, and the color, and would race it to Selma over Highway 99, cut over to Sanger, and then roar back to town down Ventura Avenue, and right smack into the very same parking space on J Street from which he had taken the car less than an hour ago.

He would stand across the street and watch the owner of the car, somebody like Dr. Cowan and his wife and two daughters, come out of Radin & Kamp where they had been shopping for an hour (he had seen them leave the car), and he would watch them get back into the car, with wrapped packages, and drive away, and not even suspect that the car had been stolen for an hour.

Wit like that.

I do not find it strange that I have been thinking about Eddie Emerian ever since he died of tuberculosis at the age of twenty, in the hospital at San Quentin Penitentiary, six months after my cousin Zav Minasian and I had taken the train from San Francisco and gone up there to say hello to Eddie and two of his pals, both of whom did a couple of years in San Quentin for armed robbery, with Eddie Emerian, and returned to Fresno to take wives and to raise families and to see grandkids.

But not Eddie. He died. It was wittier, and had more class.

And I do not find it strange that he also appears in my play *Last Chance Before the Desert*, near the end, a swift young Fresno kid chatting with the old central character of the play, myself of course.

Eddie Emerian was not only a part of my own growing up in Fresno, my own hustling of *The Herald*, my own reading of the books at the Public Library, my own watching of the people in action, he was a part of myself, as I probably was not quite a part of himself. For instance, when I discovered the magnificent physical world of Guy de Maupassant, starting with the story that both saddened and gladdened me, *The Bell*, which was also the first piece of writing that told me that my work would be to write, I took the book to Eddie and said, "Read this story, will you?" But Eddie refused to do so, saying if the story was required reading at school, he *wouldn't* read it, why should he *elect* to do so?

What I liked about him was speed, wit, and daring—life was cheap, he said, life was slow, and he was not cheap, and he could not become slow, he would never become slow, he could only be swift.

Had he not been railroaded with his two pals to the penitentiary by a stupid judge—late one night they had held up the girl selling tickets at the Hippodrome Theatre, and had taken away less than a hundred dollars, and they should have been sent home in the custody of their parents —I think Eddie Emerian would have died just the same.

He raced and he won his race. He lived his short time with his own full truth and style, power and comedy—but of course he was a damned fool, too, a much bigger damned fool than his best friend, even.

Norman Who?

ANY SON OF A BITCH comes along and writes better than I do, or makes more money, or becomes more famous, or has more girls throw themselves at him, or goes into better places in older clothes than I do, or is invited to more parties than I am, or goes on more talk shows and talks better than I do, or is admired and liked and even loved more than I am—well, any son of a bitch like that compels an instant bravo from me, just to show him that I can be big the same as any other big man, and then forever after I despise him for his impertinence.

That is only right.

There are six or seven of these writers, every one of them a fraud, a performer, a hustler, a charlatan, a con artist, a phony, a finagler, and a very boring person.

I can't stand them. They make me jealous.

I read their lousy writing and get sick to my stomach and stop reading because there is no sense to their stuff—lies, one lie after another, and all of it done in words, in college English, roller roller roller bing, rinney rinney rinney bang, rule rule rule *fflam*, on and on they go, and yet wherever smart people gather they say, "Have you read Norman's latest?"

And you say, "No, I haven't, which Norman is that?"

"Norman Amasola," they say. "Writes open letters,

sometimes to God. Have you read Norman's open letter to the Statue of Liberty, the lady with the arm held up high?"

Good old Norman Amasola, did he write a letter to Our Sweetheart of Liberty, and get us all excited all over again, like we were last year about Tennessee Waterwagon, the hillbilly poet of southwest Idaho? I love Norman, he can't write, he'll never be published, but he makes up for it in personal sincerity, high idealism, and a heart as big as a house.

Did good old Norman Amasola write a book about Norma Shearer?

Norma Talmadge?

Norma *Jean?* The *actual* name of the girl?

Is that a fact? Well, don't tell me any more about it. Please.

And here he comes, long arms dangling, he's lost his western sheriff's bow-legged approach, he sits down and smiles, and mosquito Dick Cavett says something along the line of, "Have you beat up any mounted police in Central Park lately, maybe on your way to the studio? I must explain, ladies and gentlemen, that this studio is in an old theatre just a block from Central Park and I know our friend here likes to walk, and in case he lives on Fifth Avenue, or maybe even only on Madison Avenue, above 59th Street, he could easily find his way here through Central Park at about dusk when it isn't half as dangerous as it becomes at nightfall, we tape this thing from six to half-past seven, and oh well, forget it, I can see our friend isn't enjoying this tour behind the scenes of talk shows with great American stars and personalities."

All this sort of giving of Rolls-Royce importance to various writers drives me nuts.

Even old Henry Miller gets trucked over by a Rolls-Royce limousine to where Merv Griffin does his show, wherever that is, and Merv Griffin looks right down into Henry Miller's mouth and draws back and says, "Mr. Miller, are you a dirty writer?"

And old Henry Miller says, "Well, Merv, I like your show, I *watch* your show. And wrestling. I write clean, but anybody wants to *read* dirty, let him."

It burns the bejesus out of me that these guys are keeping me in the background. Let's just please not forget that there's such a thing as ignominy.

Lillian Gish and Kitty Duval

AT THE LIBERTY THEATER in Fresno I had seen Lillian Gish in some of the nicest silent movies ever made, one of them by the great innovator David Wark Griffith: *Way Down East*.

I had also seen her in *Tol'able David*, with the title role played by that fine American lad of legend and lore Richard Barthelmess. But most unforgettable in the movie was Ernest Torrence, the supreme villain of movie dreamland, and yet even to a nine-year-old kid a grand member of the real human family. He was always in need of a shave, he looked out of his eyes with deep suspicion, which had clearly come from knowing himself, knowing what he had done and would do again at the first opportunity. He was just right in a movie containing so much tender love.

With her older sister Dorothy, Lillian Gish was a sweet and appropriate evocation of the innocence of American fantasy after the turn of the century.

And then instead of falling away and disappearing as so many others had done, as Theda Bara, and Clara Kimball Young had fallen away, for instance, Lillian Gish went right on being both a real person in the world, and a great actress, in films and plays.

Early in 1939 George Jean Nathan saw my first play, *My Heart's in the Highlands*. Now and then he'd phone

[37]

me at the Great Northern Hotel, and say something like, "I'm going to my table at 21, why don't you come by for one drink, that's all, because I've got to go back to work on my *Encyclopedia of the Theatre*."

And so I would walk over to 21 West 52nd Street and be greeted by Red on the sidewalk, and by Harry standing at the door, and by Don taking hats, and by Mac Kriendler, and by Gus the bartender, and I would go straight to the table in the corner and sit down, and George Jean Nathan would start the conversation by saying, "Girls—in all the world, is anything more amazing than girls?"

Van the corner waiter would quickly bring a big Scotch and water, which was the drink of those days, and I would take a gulp and say, "Well, they're the other half of us, at any rate."

"Not at all," Nathan would reply with his quavering voice, "they are far *more* than the other half of us, show me a man who is *anything*, and I'll show you at least three women who did it—his wife, his mother, and his daughter." Or something else just as final and just as unimportantly meaningless.

And so, on and on the easy talk would go.

In those days he spent quite a lot of time with the one American girl that I myself would have preferred had I had the good luck of having been given a choice, and one evening as we left 21, he said, "Walk with me up here a bit, I'm going to call on Lillian."

Thus, for the first time in my life, I met Lillian Gish in person, in her own apartment, which I still remember as having been like herself, a kind of self-portrait, as I suppose all places where people live are. And she was even more like a demure and shy flower than she had been in *Broken Blossoms*.

As George Jean Nathan and Lillian Gish chatted, I kept thinking, I've got to write a play for Lillian Gish.

And I did.

I wrote the part of Kitty Duval in *The Time of Your Life* for her, only to realize that a twenty-year-old San Francisco streetwalker could not be performed in 1939 by a world-famous silent-movie actress of the early 1900s. I therefore decided I had better not tell anybody that Lillian Gish had given me the idea for the heroine of my first and only money-making play.

George Jean Nathan invited me to his corner table one afternoon and introduced me to Julie Hayden, a fragile and beautiful girl he told me he just might marry, and the next time we met I suggested that she was the ideal girl to play Kitty Duval, which pleased him, and of course indeed she was, and performed the part in the original production. But I hadn't even met her when I wrote the part and the play.

Now and then when I came upon Lillian Gish somewhere I thought I ought to tell her, but I never did.

Finally, in 1969, I dedicated a book of plays to her, but the stupid, fly-by-night publisher spelled her name Lillian Gist.

I couldn't have felt more as if the situation was now totally and irrevocably hopeless, and I can only hope that this confession at last will in some small measure be the equivalent of "Lillian Gish, I love you, always have, and always will."

Hymie Myrowitz, Star
in His Own Taxi

WHENEVER I WAS FINISHED delivering or picking up tele-
grams, I would go over to the Public Library on Broadway,
across from the Orpheum Theatre, and read about various
fascinating people in the pages of a magazine called *Vanity
Fair*. It was 1924 and I was sixteen. One of the full-page
photographs in one of the issues showed very close up a
sharp young face with an expression both sly and shy in
the eyes and mouth. This was Jed Harris, a young producer
of plays, come down to New York from somewhere or
other in Connecticut, from Yale, from New Haven, and he
had already produced *Coquette* with Helen Hayes, and
The Front Page with Osgood Perkins and Lee Tracy, and
at the same time there was a third play running that Jed
Harris had produced, perhaps it was *Broadway*.

Well, of course if you didn't see Jed Harris in a full-
page photograph in *Vanity Fair*, you saw Irene Bordoni, a
singer of songs who even unseen, only heard on a phonograph record, was gorgeous. *So This Is Love?* was one of
the songs I had on a 78-rpm Victor record, and years later
I did see her in *Vanity Fair*, but with her husband, that
lucky devil—he didn't deserve her.

I did.

Or if not Irene Bordoni (whom I never so much as saw
in a show, although going into the Cub Room one night

at the Clover Club I *did* see another favorite singer, Gladys Swarthout, who used to sing the opening and closing themes of the *Firestone Hour* on radio—songs written by Mrs. Firestone, although who she was specifically I have never found out). If not Irene Bordoni, Anna Pavlova, the White Swan of the World Ballet.

They are all dead, excepting of course, Jed Harris, who has no plans to die, *at all,* most likely, but then he can't be much more than ten years older than myself. He's only seventy-seven or so.

We got into a taxi in midtown Manhattan one night in 1941 to drive over to Ben Marden's Riviera just across the George Washington Bridge, because I felt cocky and wanted to gamble and believed I would win, for I was a winner in everything else, wasn't I?

I had salvaged the play that was touring all over the country, and money was coming in every week, and everything I did was right, and everything I wrote was great, and everybody I met was famous, especially unknown people, unimportant people, real people, like taxi drivers, for instance.

Whenever I got into a New York taxi I looked at the man's photograph in the plastic frame and read his name, and now I looked at the strange desolate face of Hymie Myrowitz, in many ways not unlike the face of Jed Harris himself.

As soon as we were in the taxi Jed Harris began to say things to Hymie Myrowitz about where we were going and by what route.

I thought, This man is producing and directing this taxi ride. Is he trying to impress me, or what?

Well, of course I was a hot playwright, I had *The Time of Your Life* making money, and my first play, *My Heart's in the Highlands*, had been an artistic triumph, and so Jed

Harris was out hustling me. When he phoned me at the Hampshire House, I said, "I can't go to dinner because I'm going over to the Riviera to win some money gambling."

He replied, "I'll be by in half an hour and we'll go together, I know Ben."

Well, I *didn't* know Ben Marden, although I had been introduced to him on a previous visit to his club.

All of a sudden Jed Harris said to Hymie Myrowitz, "Listen, you stupid son of a bitch, I told you not to go up Tenth Avenue, so of course you're racing straight up Tenth Avenue, aren't you?"

Hymie Myrowitz quickly turned off Tenth Avenue and kept his mouth shut, while Jed Harris continued to insult him for being a grown man driving a dirty taxi, rolling drunks, and pimping for his wife, until finally I said, "Mr. Myrowitz, my friend is the famous Jed Harris, and he doesn't mean a word he's saying, he's only looking for some free information about how a New York taxi-driver reacts to insults—for a play he is producing, and you have given him priceless help."

The Actor in the Street

<hr>

THE FRAUD DELIGHTS my soul, and if he is big and clever and conceals his fraudulence for years, I am all the more impressed and entertained by his achievement.

As for the obvious fraud, he is impossible not to cherish, for it is a pleasant thing to see ourselves at our most absurd so openly revealed.

From the days at Emerson School when nobody was much over eleven years old, these folk heroes began to show themselves. They were the best entertainment available at the time, and many of them were Armenian, for the fact is that almost half the students at that school were Armenian, and the rest Assyrian, Irish, Portuguese, and mixed white trash.

There was a boy by the name of Aztvatzadour, which means Gift of God, who liked to speak upper-class English, saying, for instance, "I say, old fellow, where goest thou?"

Which impelled the person addressed to curse him in both Armenian and English.

His last name was Karakashian, or Stone Hauler, which suggested that among his ancestors there must have been slaves who had helped put up the Pyramids, the Tower of Babel, and other magnificent structures which time has tried in vain to efface from human memory.

Early one morning, as we stumbled in the dark on our way

to a Saturday job at the Free Market, for half a dollar, for ten hours of work, from six in the morning to three in the afternoon, he shouted, "What ho, Friar William, goest thou to the Agora? Or perhaps to the Forum? Or can it be to the Rialto?"

"Listen," I said, as he drew up beside me on Van Ness Avenue near the Fire Department, where the gate was always up revealing at first horsedrawn fire equipment ready and waiting to have the horses hitched, and then a series of great fire engines named American-La France: "Listen, Aztvatzadour, I swear to Christ, I was feeling rotten until I heard your stupid voice, but now I feel better, say some more."

But alas, not every artist is equal to applause, to being complimented, and this boy immediately fell back into himself, dropped out of his affectation, his lordly pose, and said, "You really *do* appreciate my performing, don't you, Willie? Most of the guys go fruit when I talk ancient English, but you really like it, how come?"

"I'll tell you," I said, "because I owe it to you, Aztvatzadour, let me see if I can get the last name, too, don't help me, Karakashian, that means Rock Hauler, you know, but it means a very *tired* Rock Hauler, as if for two thousand years he's been hauling the stupid rocks, I appreciate your good work in the street theatre, on the stage of life itself, so to put it, because the part you have chosen for yourself is so *wrong* for you. Go ahead and do some more, pray thee."

"Gee, Willie," he said, "thanks a lot. You're not so bad at it, either. Pray thee, not everybody says pray thee in an average conversation. But look here, there is also the church style of speech, all covered in costuming, with long red robes and great medallions hanging from long chains around the neck, you've seen and heard archbishops at our own church, saying *Dominus cantoralorus girakeyoras sourp Hayotz Bachtban yev Pirgeetch.*"

"Ah, you damned fool," I said, "you went over from good bogus Latin into classical written Armenian that even I can understand, you spoiled it, coming up with *Girakeyoras sourp Hayotz Bachtban yev Pirgeetch*, don't you know that those words actually mean Blessed Sunday, Holy Armenian Savior and Salvation?"

"No fooling?" the actor said. "I thought I was *making up* stuff, so *that's* what it was? Well, most guys would get mad at me, they wouldn't understand the words, so how come you do, Willie?"

"I don't know," I said. "Just say some more, until we get there."

But the poor fellow settled down and became big in insurance.

The Goddesses and
the Ugly Little Real Girls
of Fresno

I TENDED TO WORSHIP the girl I wanted to love, and this made trouble for me.

In the first place, feeling and believing that she was some kind of goddess made it impossible to speak to her, for how do you talk to an astonishing plump little creature of soft white flesh, thick black hair, sweet white teeth, luminous round eyes, a joyous nose with flawless nostrils, and little hands with precisely the five fingers allotted to each of them, each finger with its perfect nail, a totally innocent voice, the ability to breathe, and to speak, and to be there every single instant of the time, the same as anybody else.

Well, I just didn't find it possible to speak to such a creature, and of course it never occurred to me that it never occurred to her that she was any such thing, she was only this sweet little, neat little girl named Maxine, and any number of other boys spoke to her quite regularly, and a half dozen or more now and then even walked home with her the three or four blocks from Emerson School, and talked with her the whole way. But those poor fellows just didn't know, as I did, who they were talking to. And it didn't matter to me that she herself didn't know.

Starting at about the age of eight I wanted to have for myself, for the *rest* of myself, a girl, and in my own house, in my own life, and altogether mine, not the girl of anybody else, including surely also the girl of her father and mother.

But every girl that I wanted, apparently for that very reason, became an angel, and that prevented me from getting to speak to her at all, let alone to speak with the casual ease of others.

Thus, until a number of years later, until luck caught up with me somehow and I was able to actually approach a girl and make an effort at conversation, dry-mouthed and gulpy as it might be, I simply admired the magnificent creatures from a distance and waited. But just what was it I was waiting for?

Well, I was waiting for a synchronization: what I thought of her, I felt, should impel her both to know that it was being felt, and by *me*, and for her therefore to be or to *become* that exalted creature, and at the same time to discover me, and to know that what she was in my heart and mind as a girl I was therefore in her heart and mind as a boy: and there was no mistake about it, she was a goddess to me, I was a god to her, and it was true, it was no lie, it was the simplest reality, or why would I have discovered her divinity in the first place?

I didn't invent it out of thin air. It was there in her, and I was enchanted by it and even hushed and astonished by it, by the enormity and magnificence of it, and there was surely in a boy who saw a girl that way something in himself of a like order, in the dimension of maleness.

But no girl discovered me, as I had discovered so many of them, in total secrecy, since to tell them of the discovery would be pathetic, and something they would not be able to understand, or be equal to, in any case.

Finally, I took to trying to get home, so to put it, without all of the beauty, truth, glory, magnificence, and grandeur that I had discovered in the female. I didn't like the loss, but

I also didn't insist that it was fatal—that is, it didn't deprive me of the need to get home, at any rate.

And so sitting behind me at Fresno High School a kind of rich girl named Lois Craighead one day softly sang almost into my ear a song by Irving Berlin entitled *It Had to Be You.*

I turned around and looked at her skinny, rather silly, rather ugly face—she loved to eat lobster, she had written in a class paper—and she half-smiled and nodded, and although she was not the girl I wanted to get to at all, I felt deeply moved by her roundabout declaration of discovery of me. And although I never pursued the idea, I have always felt that she was a very important woman in my life.

On the Way to *Who's Who*

I WAS WANDERING through the streets of Fresno, in a kind of afternoon amnesia, trying to sell *The Evening Herald* about a month after I had started selling papers every day, before I had earned the right to have a corner, a right that was based upon the number of papers sold every day *without* a corner, and then I was loitering outside Homan's Sport Goods Store looking at the red, gold, and black lures in which hooks were cleverly fixed to deceive great fish, and I was dreaming about fishing on a riverbank somewhere and bringing in a beautiful fish, as if it might be a kind of prize from heaven, or from art itself, and then suddenly I remembered that I had ten papers to sell, to earn the day's quarter, to continue to maintain my chance of soon winning a corner, and so turned away from the dreaming and began hustling again, saying to anybody walking by, "Paper, mister? Paper, lady?"

But there were very few women walking the streets of Fresno unaccompanied, not even streetwalkers, who either stood in one place, looking like original deception itself, as grand as any red, gold, and black fish lure ever was, or strolled about with their pimps, or boyfriends, for if a young Armenian had himself a working girl, as the saying was, she was not a whore, and he was not a pimp, she was a working girl and he was her lover, and they both cared a lot about appearances and wore very stylish clothes.

Consequently, I soon enough gave up trying to sell a paper to a woman, or at any rate to try to hustle her into buying one. You sold papers to men, not women. You hustled men. You admired women. You revered, you loved them.

You asked a man if he wanted a paper. If he remained undecided, you mentioned the day's big news, and *that* was hustling. If one out of fifty bought a paper, you were doing just fine.

On Van Ness Avenue that dreamy afternoon in 1916, about two months after I had left the Fred Finch Orphanage, and had gone home to Fresno, to my own family, transferred from an orderly institution into a disorderly household, and had begun to become an Armenian, like it or not, to accept the reality and to make the most of it, and had effaced the orphanage from memory, as if I hadn't spent five years there, I hustled a skinny well-dressed man coming down the street, saying, "Paper, mister?"

The man stopped, smiled, and said, "Aren't you William? Aren't you Willie? Saroyan?"

Well, of course I was, but I was also dreaming, I was also selling papers, I was also anonymous, as all newsboys are, a newsboy is a newsboy, he is not somebody named, and being named seemed to me to constitute something very nearly like fame or trouble, why should anybody know my name unless he was in the family, or one of the people at Emerson School? Was this man possibly some kind of cop, for in those very first days of selling papers I was afraid of cops, first of all because it was supposed to be against some kind of law for any boy under ten to sell papers, and in fact most of the boys were more than ten years old, usually twelve or thirteen, after which they stopped, unless they looked small. And then I was afraid of cops because they had power and I had seen them use it on Indians and drunks.

Well, if he was a cop, what had I done wrong? Had he been observing me? Was it against some kind of law to stand and study the fish lures in Homan's window and to dream of bringing in a salmon from the San Joaquin River at Mendota?

But honesty has always been an uncontrollable reflex of my nature, and speed has been the only reaction to anything that confronts me, and so I said, "Yes sir."

"I *thought* so," the man said. "I used to see you up at the orphanage. Do you remember me? Edgar Ellis, manager of the laundry? When you kids put on little plays and charged a pin admission you used to come down to the laundry and ask me for pins, and I'd get out the tray in which we kept pins, and buttons, and even sometimes a penny that had fallen out of somebody's pocket. How's everything here in Fresno?"

I didn't know what to tell the man, but I felt famous for having been so specifically remembered. I didn't have even a vague memory of him. And as for how everything was, there just wasn't any way even to begin to say.

But speed is speed, so I said, "Just fine, thank you."

And he said, "Do you remember me?" And I instantly knew courtesy would justify the lie and said, "Oh, yes, Mr. Ellis."

And then and there I was famous.

How Can Anybody Like a Man Who Says He Never Met a Man He Didn't Like?

THE COWBOY BOGUS-BOOB Will Rogers enjoyed a lot of sickening fame for his coy head-down chewing-gum pronouncements about human politics, looking up at the world like an Arab girl to her betrothed. And he accepted as if it were a statement he had actually made to somebody in real life, and not the invention of a gag-writer or a publicity agent, "I never met a man I didn't like."

Bogus-boob, because he was cleverer than any slicker on Broadway itself, but kept up the pose for the rest of his life—that is to say, a hick from Oklahoma, part-Indian, so what did he know about anything?

Well, he knew enough to be a star of Ziegfeld's Follies for a long time, at top wages, and he knew enough to do a brief daily feature for a lot of U.S. daily papers. He was also smart enough to be invited everywhere by everybody, and to accept, and to go right on carrying on as if he were just this hayseed feller from down by the barn and bronco-busting ring.

And so somebody sent out H. Allen Smith as a young newspaper reporter to meet the man who had never met anybody he didn't like.

And years later, H. Allen Smith wrote a magazine piece about this adventure: Will Rogers hated H. Allen Smith on sight, he loathed H. Allen Smith before he met him, he had nothing but contempt for H. Allen Smith when H. Allen Smith telephoned him, he wanted to bust H. Allen Smith in the mouth when H. Allen Smith tried to be a good reporter and tried to force a meeting with the great American legendary saint. When H. Allen Smith finally did catch up with Will Rogers, the gentle cowboy scarcely looked at him and snarled, "Get away from me boy, you bother me."

Now, this is not meant to belittle Will Rogers, because he needs no outside assistance. And in any case, I never met him, I never saw him in person anywhere, I never saw him in the Ziegfeld Follies or in vaudeville or in a rodeo or leading a Pasadena New Year's Day Parade, or in any other actual living reality. I once saw him in a movie named *Jubilo*, or something like that. I was ten or eleven, and I thought the rube was great, but then I thought anybody in the movies was great, and they *were*, flickering to the pipe-organ music of the Liberty Theatre.

I never found anything written by Will Rogers authentic in any way at all. And so my regard, or disregard, for him is at least pure.

But I did meet H. Allen Smith while I was on a visit to Hollywood in 1936. He was no big bargain, either, but he *may* be remembered for believing he knew the best recipe for Texas chili con carne, which I very much doubt.

Whatever Happened
to Jim Lundy?

BUT WHAT did we want, what did each of us want, so many
of us now dead, so many of us now dying, so few of us
still roaring?

We wanted our greatness not to be secret. We wanted
it known to the world at large, to the rest of the human
family, not just to our own little family.

Back of 2226 San Benito Avenue, somewhere south on
M Street, up toward the Fresno Brewery, built of brick,
Bavarian in architecture, beautiful, austere, a touch of
Europe in our midst, a castle on the spur of the Southern
Pacific Railroad, and not of the Rhine, back where the
houses continued pretty much the way they were on San
Benito and on I, J, K, and L Streets, but where there were
also smaller houses fitted in here and there, as space allowed,
there lived a young man whose name was Jim Lundy,
whose fame with all of us was enormous both as an athlete
and as a man who walked the sidewalk of the world: he
was famous, that is, to Henry and Willie Saroyan, to Ralph
and Yep Moradian, who occupied the house across the
alley from our house. And over at the corner of San
Benito and M, Jim Lundy enjoyed the admiration of
Yeghish and Vahan Shekoyan. And then up M Street,
Andreas Bazoyan's two boys, Vahan and Suren, lived in a
house near where Jim Lundy slept and ate some of his
meals, although nobody seemed to know very much about
the matter. All of us were from Bitlis, in the Armenian
highlands, and the time was the last year of the World

War, 1918. We were about ten years old, the kid brothers of us, and the big brothers around thirteen. And Jim Lundy couldn't have been more than eighteen, or he would have been drafted as everybody else had been.

He appeared in the morning, moving like a tiger, lithe, hard, supple, swift, and with that unmistakable grace of the great man that informs younger men, also great, here he is, here is the model in the world, never mind the father, if you have one on the scene, never mind the mother's kid brother, or the father's kid brother, if they also happen to be on hand, never mind the members of the family, Jim Lundy is the model of the powerful man who is of the whole world itself.

One day I saw Jim Lundy coming home at dusk of a March evening, while Vahan Shekoyan and I were pegging an indoor baseball at each other to see who could take the peg and not suddenly need to step away from it. Our hands were already red and swelling from the stings they had taken in that game. I scarcely let Jim Lundy's eye catch mine when I pegged the ball at him, fair and square, from not much more than twenty feet with all my might. Well, he very casually let the ball come to his hands, and then wound up to throw the ball back, continuing the game, and drove me not so much into flinching, or stepping out of the way, as into resignation to destruction, but the ball somehow came to me without a tenth of the force which his motion had suggested.

I caught it, and he half-laughed and said, "Good throw, good catch, Willie."

There was a great man.

He even knew my name.

And he was real to all of us for only a year or two.

Whatever happened to Jim Lundy from down M Street somewhere?

The Baltimore Bad Boy

VERY EARLY along in my reading of American writing I came upon *Prejudices* by H. L. Mencken. I was both delighted and instructed in matters of honest manners and formal art—rather than the art that a growing boy tends to notice and admire in the human race at large. That is to say, the simple art of being, of having character, of having style, street style if you prefer, involving stance, posture, eye, leg, foot, arm, hand, voice, speech, entrances and exits, and the whole participation in the continuous drama upon a given stage—home, school, church, Public Library, Civic Auditorium, street.

There was, and there always had been, a choice for a man to make about himself, and about everybody else, and therefore his relationship or connection to them.

At church, one of the great unknowns and unknowables was of course the central character, and I saw no reason to repudiate him, to resent him, or to doubt his message, although I also didn't see any reason to make as much of him in all dimensions of my own life as the church thought I should.

H. L. Mencken, on the other hand, found it both desirable and amusing to attack all who earnestly took to Jesus, or pretended to, for he found them mainly American businessmen looking for bigger profits. They used Christianity to gain wealth and power.

In exposing these people, H. L. Mencken made me laugh —sometimes out loud, in the reading room of the Public Library on Broadway in Fresno, with the various library workers looking up at me in shades of astonishment, gratitude, disbelief, and gentle annoyance. Mustn't laugh in the Public Library, you know, as I had a character say years later in a play called *Jim Dandy*.

H. L. Mencken was a Baltimore man, writing for the *Sun*, who had moved out into the world of magazine publishing with the *Smart Set*, a magazine just enough before my time not to be a part of my reading experience. But when with George Jean Nathan he founded *The American Mercury*, I studied the first issue in 1924 from cover to cover at the Public Library. Writing on an Underwood upright typewriter at 3204 El Monte Way, I began to send him essays, which came back in terrible silence in the self-addressed stamped envelope, each manuscript with a clipped-on printed Rejection Slip. Not a word from H. L. Mencken himself, not a word from George Jean Nathan, not a word from even a clerk at *The American Mercury*.

And there I was sixteen full years of age getting nowhere. But how could I get anywhere? The stuff I sent out was bad. One of the essays had the title *Your High School Ignoramus Speaks*, which may suggest how sad the writing was, but perhaps also the unfortunate effect of Mr. Mencken's style on one raw, inexperienced new writer in a small and barren place of America.

I kept trying to break into *The American Mercury* all through 1924 and 1925, and then I got mad and wrote an attack on *Mencken, Nathan, Haldeman-Julius, and God*— but neither *The Bookman, Scribner's, The North American*

Review, Century, nor any of the other quality magazines wanted the thing. Need I add, the dirty rats? I just couldn't break into the writing game, as I had heard it put in various advertisements of correspondence schools. I never took anybody's course, and I never stopped reading H. L. Mencken. He was just too funny, too good a writer, to lose simply because he had no time to notice that if my writing was bad, there was surely at least a *hint* of real genius between the lines. He certainly discovered a couple of interesting writers while they were still young, why not me? And then I decided, Ah the hell with it, I'll only enjoy reading *The American Mercury* every month, I won't even *try* to write for it.

That was a very intelligent decision.

And then all of a sudden things began to happen. I was in, I was no longer out, and I had even had a couple of stories in *The American Mercury* itself, even though it was no longer edited by H. L. Mencken. But at least the format was the same, the green cover, and the paper, and the print.

We finally met at his home on Hollins Street in Baltimore. He looked precisely like a German butcher's boy, although his father was actually a German cigar-maker.

We had a nice lunch, served by his housekeeper and cook, and then he lighted up a cigar while I continued to smoke Chesterfields—pure nicotine and tar, but in those days also pure pleasure.

Some of the things he said at lunch are still vivid in my mind, and while I know he didn't mean anything literally, he also didn't qualify any of his remarks, and didn't smile or wink or otherwise seek to let me know not to take him too seriously.

I didn't, in any case, because what he said was clearly art, not history.

I must have mentioned Theodore Roosevelt with something like respect, most likely because I had spent time reading around in Theodore Roosevelt's book *African Game Trails*, a copy of which had been in our house from the time I was eight. I was therefore surprised when H. L. Mencken said, "A monster. A bully. A fraud. A coward. Even his voice was false, he talked with a high falsetto, and when he tried to throw his weight around in arriving somewhere you could see that he was *working* at it, he was putting his feet down *deliberately* heavily, announcing his arrival. It was pathetic."

Well, I thought, maybe that was the way the man walked, that's all.

"Well," I said, "I don't know how he walked, but he was certainly a great horseman leading the Rough Riders up San Juan Hill."

Mencken puffed neatly at his cigar, let a little smoke move through his nostrils, put some of it out of his mouth neatly, and then said, "He never *saw* San Juan Hill. They showed it to him on a map in his room at the U.S. Embassy in Havana. No, if you want to admire a politician, at least choose somebody worthwhile."

"Lincoln?" I suggested.

"Abraham?" Mencken said. "Good heavens, no. A psychotic, he never grew up, he was mentally ill all his life, he used to throw himself on that poor girl's grave and cry for hours. He didn't even know he wasn't really crying for her."

"Who was he crying for?" I said.

"Do you know," Mencken said, "I'm not sure? I've given the matter a lot of thought, but I haven't been able to satisfy myself. I've asked the specialists at Johns Hopkins, but they're not too bright, either. They seem to feel that it was

Lincoln's character to feel deep sorrow, which had to be released in tears *somewhere* now and then, and so he went to that grave and let it all out."

I thought better than to suggest George Washington, and so I said, "I've always had a warm feeling about Andrew Jackson."

"What in the world for?"

"Well, in American History at Longfellow Junior High School," I said, "he was lying under a shade tree during some war or other, eating acorns because there was nothing else to eat, and along came a tired private and flopped down beside him. Well, General Andrew Jackson gave that unknown soldier *three* of his five acorns. And of course the soldier never knew that his benefactor had been the great Andrew Jackson."

H. L. Mencken said softly, "It never happened. He was a very bad general, and a worse president. It was traditional when the school history books were being written to throw in a few anecdotes like that, but they were all invariably false and silly."

"Well, who then?" I said.

"I rather think you might have enjoyed Warren Gamaliel Harding," H. L. Mencken said. "The Teapot Dome Scandal wasn't his fault, he just didn't know how to tell his rich friends not to make a public fool of him. And of course he was a *born* fool. That's why I rather liked him. He died of heartburn, you know."

Well, of course I knew that he had suddenly died at the Palace Hotel in San Francisco under mysterious circumstances, but rather than play straight man for H. L. Mencken I said, "I never could understand why William Jennings Bryan couldn't win an election."

H. L. Mencken said, "Well, if you had been out to Dayton, Kentucky, at the time of the Monkey Trial, as it was called, you might really have had *reason* to wonder why he hadn't been elected President, for he was never so stupid as out there, and the people loved him, all the voters out there loved him, he was their boy. I was the enemy, and they hated me, and that's how it was all over the country. If he had lived, he would have won the next election. But he ate too much. He was always eating. Poor fellow, I really liked him. He *smelled* Christian, you know. Sweaty." And on and on old H. L. Mencken went in 1941, a delightful old religious fanatic all the way.

The Girl of the World Who Disappeared Forever inside Turk Street

THE 1920S WERE MAGNIFICENT years for me, for in the year 1920 I pretty much left boyhood, the rock-hard erection had arrived, the orgasm in sleep had arrived, the hand reaching down, as James Agee once said, a million years to the hot stick of the male night, had arrived, the significance of the scent of female bodies had arrived, and everything had suddenly shifted from innocence, unaware-ness, indifference, neutrality into a complicated, powerful, and troublesome potential, full of the possibility for either of the opposites, pleasure or pain, effectiveness or ineffec-tuality, health or disease, and we might as well acknowledge that the possibility of clap and syphilis was made to be terri-fying by such people as coaches at school, Sunday School teachers, and athletic directors at the Y.M.C.A. Whenever we went there on a Saturday morning for a free swim, there was first always the syphilis lecture, with colored charts of the human body, and pictures of healthy and diseased genitals. And if it was not put forward that masturbation caused insanity, certainly Coach Battersby at Longfellow School did say that it destroyed many a great athletic career.

The summer my genitals flared up, and itched, my grand-mother Lucy, who had a lot of common sense, one evening in private made me sit in a corrugated tin tub full of cold water, and sure enough the genitals cooled off. But later when I went to a doctor for a salve or something, he asked, "How often do you masturbate?" And seemed astonished that I honestly replied, "I don't." Of course I had, but only a couple of times, which hardly counted.

The orgasm disconnected from its proper destination just didn't really ever appeal to me, and I felt right in saving myself for my own girl, whoever she might be. In the early 1930s the search for her was not discontinued, and if anything was intensified, but now I had come around to believing that there was something also to be said for the enjoyment of other girls and women, including the working girls of the various San Francisco houses, one of whom one night seemed so beautiful that I was plunged into despair about human life itself, about the position of women in the world, and into mourning for the loss of the girl I had been seeking all my life.

For this girl *did* seem to be the one I had been waiting for. She was beautiful beyond anything seen by me anywhere before—at school, in the streets, behind counters in department stores, in movies, on the stage, at church.

This was the one, and she was a two-dollar whore at a place on Turk Street near Leavenworth. Before I could choose her to go with me to a private room, she was called away by the young madam, Rosalie. I refused to have another girl, and told Rosalie I would be back, and left the place with one of my Fresno friends of those days, a former prizefighter, an Armenian, who boxed under the name of Kid Jazz.

An hour later when we went back I asked Rosalie to bring out the black-haired beauty in the red velvet dress. She brought out six girls, but my girl was not among them.

Rosalie insisted that she had had no other girl, but Kid Jazz walking in the street said he also had seen her during our first visit but not during our second, so what had happened to her? Had she indeed *been* one of the six girls during our second visit, but in only one hour had so changed as to have disappeared forever?

Browsing at Bill McDevitt's Bookstore in 1929

BILL MCDEVITT OWNED a big shambling cluttered bookstore in San Francisco on Sutter Street above Fillmore, and I used to go in there and browse, because print and publication, paper and binding, title page and margin, and all the rest of the business and reality of language in action has always seemed near to where I ought to be, something like my home, and my way.

He was a skinny man of about sixty-six, I suppose, when I was twenty, and just back from New York, early in 1929, still a failure, an unpublished writer, brooding about it, and therefore open to the invitation of books that had not failed, of names that were on title pages, of writers who were not anonymous.

In addition to the daily visit to the Public Library in the Civic Center I went to Bill McDevitt's to browse at the crowded tables, loaded with dusty books, pamphlets, brochures and English language paperbacks published in Europe. In those days there were no paperback American books, and indeed not more than six years later I published an essay in *The New Republic* pointing out the absurd exclusivity of books, much too expensive for the working man. A novel was two dollars, other books were anywhere from three to five dollars, and my argument was that good books should be twenty-five cents.

Old Bill McDevitt knew every item in his shop, which had a kind of T shape: from floor to ceiling were shelves filled with books, books on the tables, and books on the floors, generally in corners.

If you went to the old man, as he leaned somewhere reading something, or running through a new batch of stuff he had bought, and if you said, "What about Ambrose Bierce? Do you have the *Devil's Dictionary?* I was just reading it at the Public Library and I'll buy it if it doesn't cost too much," old Bill would look at you, lifting his spectacles, silver-framed, and reply, "No, I don't have the *Devil's Dictionary*, but I have *In the Midst of Life.* It's from the Nash edition of his collected works, very fine paper and binding, so it isn't cheap, but I'll let you have it for a dollar."

And I would say, "That's too much for me, but I'd like to *look* at the book, at any rate."

And he would say, "Well, I think I know where it is." And he would go over to a table piled high with all kinds of books, and he would fish in among them, and tug out a heavy book, open it, and then slam it shut to make the dust fly, and then he would wipe the rest of the dust from the book with a large red bandana he kept in his back pocket, and he would turn to the title page, and then he would hand the book to me and say, "You'll notice that it's priced at five dollars—well, to a collector that wouldn't be too much at all, and he'd be glad to have it, but I doubt if you're a collector."

"Yes sir," I would say, "you're right, I am not a collector."

"Well," he would say, "as you can see, I am. I am a collector of books and anything else in that line—maps, drawings, prints, songs."

And like as not, he would pick up a piece of sheet music

of the 1890s and sing something along the lines of *Didn't You Know He's the Dandiest Dandy of Old Danbury Road.* And then he would mumble something and return to his place, while I stood and examined the handsome book of Ambrose Bierce's weird short stories—stories of unaccountable events among human beings.

Visiting old Bill McDevitt's bookshop three blocks from the family flat at 2378 Sutter Street, at the corner of Divisadero, was part of the whole business of being connected to paper and print, words and punctuation marks, language and books. But the place was also unbearably sad and depressing, something like a neglected graveyard under heavy rain.

John Fante, on a visit one afternoon, suddenly said: "Let's get out of here, this place makes writing seem stupid, and being a writer ridiculous."

Doughbelly's Crap Game
on the Embarcadero

WORKING AT DODD WAREHOUSE across from Pier 17 in San Francisco, during my lunch hours I used to wander among the railroad tracks and boxcars of the waterfront, and there one day I found a crap game in progress, owned and operated by a big black man who was called Doughbelly.

I was twenty, one of four clerks working for three dollars a day. Our boss was a man named Henry Savage whose character was precisely the opposite of his name, a man of not more than thirty, who gently instructed men almost twice his age in little bookkeeping chores, and instructed me in more physical chores, such as going on errands to various places nearby.

Doughbelly had surely been a longshoreman, unloading cargoes, doing easy work for a big man, but had lately retired, and had established his own waterfront crap game.

He took a modest cut from every pot, surely less than ten percent, perhaps as little as one percent if the pot got big.

When I dropped a silver dollar to fade a man coming out for a first roll, Doughbelly looked up and said, "Where you from?"

Well, I was in a ready-made gray herringbone suit I had bought in New York for eleven dollars in late August of the previous year, 1928, and I was clearly not a longshoreman, so he probably wanted to know where I worked, for this was strictly a local lunchtime crap game, lasting from about 11:30 to about 1:30.

Without thinking I said, "New York." The result was that the next day during my lunch hour when I showed up he said, "Here comes New York."

The longshoremen were soon identifying me as the New York Kid, and when years later I began to gamble in the famous poker parlor called The Menlo Club on Turk Street I was known by that name, probably transferred there by one or another of the longshoremen I had rolled dice with in the lunchtime games managed by Doughbelly.

He was a workingman, a longshoreman, a man who was very black and yet somehow not African-looking, and he had ease, authority, intelligence, and superiority.

I lost my day's wages (and then some) for about a week, and then I decided I had better not answer the challenge of the rolling dice any more, for I was expected to contribute something to the family fund for expenses—rent, food, laundry, good God, the very words still make me cringe and laugh, for I heard them every day chanted by everybody in the family in a litany of righteousness, whenever I was out of work: rent, food, laundry: rent, food, laundry.

For years I found it impossible to pass up a chance to bet that my luck would be better than the luck of anybody else. In the waterfront lunchtime crap games, almost invariably I started out by winning very nicely, imagined I might make a score, and wound up losing back both what I had won and all of the money in my possession.

Doughbelly noticed this and without speaking seemed to puzzle over it.

One day he said, "Why don't you quit when you're ahead?"

"I'm never ahead enough."

He smiled and nodded, and I knew he understood what I was really talking about. It wasn't crapshooting, it was everything, especially writing.

But of course I never said, "I'm a writer." I *was* a writer. I wasn't published, that's all. You are a writer when other people know it in the only way that such a thing may be known: by having your writing in print. I just didn't have a book of my own, although I seemed to have all of the books of the world going through me all the time.

The Man from Matador, Texas

STANLEY ROSE WAS from Matador, Texas, and he was the owner of a bookshop in Hollywood where movie people dropped by to browse and to chat.

How he had ever got the notion of opening a bookshop I never did find out, but there he was, seemingly serene and perfectly at home everywhere, but especially in his shop, buying books from the salesmen of publishers and selling them to people in the *industry*, as they themselves used to put it, and he in turn with a little mischief in his voice used to put it, too.

I began to visit his shop long before I became a published writer. At that time, in the early 1930s, the shop was on Vine Street next door to Levy's Restaurant, down a hundred yards from the Plaza Hotel. Across the street from the Plaza stood the Brown Derby. It was a good location.

Every afternoon Stanley Rose filled a satchel with new books and visited three or four studios, to show the books to producers, directors, writers, and even to actors and actresses, although he didn't think any of them ever really read any book they bought.

I therefore asked if *he* ever did, and he said with his slow Texas speech, "Well, not all the way through maybe, but I know what every book in the shop *is*."

He had been a con man, he had also been a bootlegger,

and in his early days in Hollywood, before opening the bookstore, he had done a little time. He had also dealt in what he called dirty books.

He seemed to be able to speak about his past as if it really hadn't been shabby at all, or as if it hadn't involved himself. He certainly hadn't reformed, he had only grown into other activities.

He once took upon himself another man's guilt, and went to jail for six months. His friends told me that he did the time for a well-known writer, but what the details were I never learned. When I brought the matter up, Stanley Rose didn't deny that it had happened, he just didn't go into detail, since it involved somebody else.

His lease on the Vine Street place ran out, and he found a place three or four blocks up from Vine on Hollywood Boulevard next door to Musso and Frank's famous chop and steak house, where at the counter you saw the good charcoal fire sizzling the good beef and lamb.

Stanley liked to drink, and now and then the consequences of many years of drinking put him into the Veterans' Hospital from whence he nevertheless several times phoned me to smuggle him a bottle of Old Crow, which I did of course. He died comparatively young, fifty-five or so, but there was no big Hollywood funeral for him, although he knew everybody and the truth about everybody in Cinema City, as he sometimes put it.

For twenty years or so, from the time I met him to the time he died, he was one of my best friends. Saying so long to him one night at four, he said, "It's lonely." And he went stumbling up the daybreak street.

Yvor Winters and His Poetry Students at Stanford

Edward J. O'Brien—the very name in print, to my eye, means the Short Story—started bringing out a book called *The Best American Short Stories* when I was seven or eight years old. In 1915, I believe.

I discovered the series when I was eleven or twelve, and went through each book and studied the supplementary material at the back of each of them: especially the biographical notes, and the names and addresses of magazines: to this day a fascinating series of books, one of the best ideas ever to happen to American writing, for the short story seems to be the form we like best, as it is surely the form that the Irish like best, for one, and the Russians for another, and the French, for a third.

Well, Edward J. O'Brien published *Resurrection of a Life* by Sirak Goryan in his book, about the year 1935, twenty years after the series started. The story had first appeared in the Armenian English-language weekly *Hairenik*, published in Boston.

Sirak Goryan, however, was William Saroyan, writing out of the front room of the second floor flat at 348 Carl Street in San Francisco.

Why Sirak Goryan? I wanted the name to be Armenian, I had several cousins named Sirak, and Goryan was the name of an eighth-century writer of Armenia—it was his pen name, as a matter of fact, and it means Lion Cub. Actually the name is Goriun, and I had heard that he was not an ecclesiastical writer but a worldly, a people's writer.

In the meantime, William Saroyan had had a short story accepted by *Story* magazine in December of 1933 and published in the February 1934 issue, *The Daring Young Man on the Flying Trapeze.*

Well, Edward J. O'Brien received a letter from his friends Whit Burnett and Martha Foley about *The Daring Young Man on the Flying Trapeze* by this new writer in San Francisco, an ethnic Armenian, as the saying is. O'Brien replied that he also had discovered an ethnic Armenian writer, Sirak Goryan.

And so of course when he wrote to William Saroyan saying that he wanted to publish *The Daring Young Man on the Flying Trapeze,* I replied that I was indeed both Sirak Goryan (henceforth dead) and William Saroyan (henceforth not dead).

Before this particular time, from the back pages of one of O'Brien's annuals, I had found out about a magazine called *Gyroscope,* which was published in Palo Alto, and so I sent that magazine a poem entitled *Christ at the Seal Pool* (in the court of the Aquarium at Golden Gate Park).

The editor wrote that *Gyroscope* was a mimeographed (almost private) publication which had been discontinued, in any case, but he liked the poem and would I visit his house next Friday at four o'clock for tea and to meet some of his students at Stanford. Signed, Yvor Winters.

I took the train, following his instructions, phoned from the station, he came by in five minutes, and I met a friendly, stern, stocky man about ten years older than me, thirty-two to my twenty-two that is—a poet and a professor.

We reached his little house almost out in the country, and I heard, smelled, and saw goats. And when we went inside he introduced me to his wife Janet Lewis, and then to some of his students: Achilles Holt of Texas, who either died a few years later in a car accident or committed suicide; Henry Ramsey about whom I remember very little; Bunichi Kagawa who said that James Joyce's *Ulysses* was being translated into Japanese; J. V. Cunningham; and several young women.

Tea was served and my cup did a little tap dance in the saucer: I had never met people like Yvor Winters and Janet Lewis and their friends.

But the filled cup was emptied and filled again, and the second time the tap dancing wasn't so wild and loud.

They had an infant daughter to whom Janet Lewis dedicated a novel entitled *The Invasion*, calling the daughter Little Red Feather.

And a few years later in Pasadena, I met Yvor Winters' brother-in-law, Wessell Smitter, a writer as well as a tree man, so to put it: he supplied full-grown trees of all kinds to rich retired people who didn't have time to set out new trees in their gardens.

Yvor Winters was the first real writer I ever met. He was an austere soul, with a hard unyielding intelligence, and he demanded that poetry be great, that's all.

He told me he had received several very long typewritten letters from an unknown poet named Kenneth Rexroth, did I by any chance know him?

No, but of course not long afterwards I met Rexroth, who is one of the marvels and paradoxes of San Francisco, the United States, and very likely the world.

Yvor Winters was a great man for me to meet at that moment, and I pay homage to his memory.

The Fragile Sensitive Writer
and the Mean Old World

HENRY MILLER WROTE to me from Paris, in care of Random
House, who forwarded the letter to 348 Carl Street, in
San Francisco. I had never heard of him. Everybody is
named Miller, and very nearly everybody is named Henry
Miller.

I was twenty-six years old. My first book had made a
very good beginning for me as a writer, and quite a few
writers had written to me, some famous, some ignored, some
unpublished, and so the letter from Henry Miller was interesting only in that it had come from Paris, and possibly also
because he said that I was the only real writer in the United
States.

Well, actually there were several real writers. As a matter
of fact, there were several *dozen* of them, including the
eventual winners of the Nobel Prize: Eugene O'Neill,
whom I had never met, whose daughter Oona in 1941
came out from New York with her friend who became my
wife, and the responsibility for getting them about both in
Hollywood and in San Francisco fell to me and to my
Cadillac convertible with the top down—which caused
Oona's big floppy hat as she was traveling away from her
first meeting with Charles Chaplin, at that time involved in
paternity litigation with a perfectly nice girl named Joan
Barry, I believe, to fly off her head like a large bird, making me draw up at the side of the highway and run back
a hundred yards to retrieve it. And then when we stopped

at the El Tejon Hotel in Bakersfield, in memory of the great summers I had known there, working with my mother's kid brother Aram in the shipping of the first California grapes, from the Southern Pacific siding called Magunden, and ordered ham and eggs and coffee and rye toast for each of us, Oona piped up in her sweet voice, "May I have some ketchup, too, please?" The waiter fetched her a bottle and she used it all before she was done with the meal, impelling me to call her the high-pitched ketchup kid, which means absolutely nothing. Her father virtually turned her away from his door at his Contra Costa home, along with her friend the future bride. Later Chaplin said, "I don't like his playwriting. I think it is very dull."

In any case, Eugene O'Neill probably deserved the Nobel Prize, and got it long before Charles Chaplin gave his verdict.

Sherwood Anderson was passed over in favor of one of his many admirers, or even students, or should I say two— I meant to say William Faulkner, who clearly acknowledged his debt to the old flabby boy of magnificent indecision and longing, and I speak with admiration, not scorn. And Ernest Hemingway, who ridiculed the master in *Torrents of Spring*, and never seemed able or willing to acknowledge any kind of literary debt to anyone, certainly not to Gertrude Stein, who plump and pompous as she was, with her devoted and worshipful Alice B. Toklas nearby, really did a great deal for the young Mr. Hemingway that is evident in both his earliest and best work and in his later and more (or slightly more) mature work—and yet he came to despise the dumpy lesbian, as he might as well have put it in *A Moveable Feast*, in which he avoided speaking about Sherwood Anderson at all.

These were real writers, and they one by one accepted the Nobel Prize: O'Neill, Hemingway, and Faulkner.

Furthermore, when Henry Miller wrote to tell the young writer at 348 Carl Street in San Francisco that he was the only real writer in America, Thomas Wolfe was very much alive, and only thirty-five years old. And there was something to be said for a good assortment of other writers.

Even so, in replying to Henry Miller I didn't say, "Aw, shucks, man, I'm not the only real writer in America, I'm only the best one." I just sort of accepted the absurd theory and put into the letter another couple of hundred (or was it thousand?) words, out of youth and happiness—for indeed I did reply to everybody in those days, and every reply was more of a story, a work of art, than just a letter to somebody I didn't know. And I didn't start to make carbon copies of letters until ten years later (on the advice of lawyers, for God's sake, not literary people at all).

The first thing I knew, two or three or four letters had been exchanged with Henry Miller, and there in Paris was this big crybaby of a man, aged forty-six to my twenty-six asking me to please, please immediately round up some cash and send it to him by airmail special delivery, he was desperate.

Well, I thought, fuck him, I'm a writer, and I've been anywhere he's been, in the money department, and I've never begged in my life, so why does he put the bite on me?

This was the end of the celebrated Miller-Saroyan correspondence. I didn't send him any money, and he didn't write again.

Years later he told a reporter, "We thought Saroyan was a tiger, but he wasn't."

He also sent the San Francisco sculptor Beniamino Bufano to my door on Taraval Street in 1945 with one of Henry Miller's watercolors, for only $100. I wrote out a check but sent back the painting—a half-nude that I considered middle class and boring.

Fame and Fortune and Fun at the Hampshire House

As soon as I began to be in the money I took to living like a millionaire, which I had always wanted to do, just to see how it felt.

It felt fine, there was nothing like it, but I have always had this foolish inability not to notice that not everybody, not even writers, not even good ones, can suddenly get in the money and live like millionaires, and so this knowledge sometimes embarrassed me and sometimes made me feel a fraud, although I had earned my money the hard way, taking great risks, and never knowing if I could earn a meagre living, let alone a fortune.

Even after you've won fame and fortune, every time you write you've got to write, there's no shortcut, you have to start your career all over again.

I felt a fraud because how could I enjoy my success, my fame and fortune, when this good luck did nothing at all for anybody else, other than, of course, members of my immediate family, and friends, and those strangers I happened to chance upon and was impelled to hand a few dollars to, after which I felt worse than ever, for what could a few dollars possibly do for a man who was unfit for this world and yet unable to make a world of his own, which is of course what pretty much every writer does, as Mr. Bernard Shaw himself pointed out a long time ago.

I think Shaw's comment was part of an attack upon psychiatry, and the theory that it is a kind of illness for a man not to adjust to reality, to the real world.

Nonsense, Shaw said, why should any man adjust to such disorder and meaninglessness, unless he is indeed terribly sick?

In any case, while the flush and fun of success had not yet turned to something like anger and sorrow, I lived like the rich people do, and so I took a suite overlooking Central Park at the Hampshire House, at that time probably the swankiest place in New York, but with real class, everything designed by Dorothy Draper, as I was informed.

I even had patent-leather loafing slippers, a silk lounging robe, and the very best clothes and shoes. The only reason I didn't have money lying around all over the place was because I had been informed by a man named Pat Duggan, whose mother was a Christian Science practitioner and had both worked and witnessed fantastic miracles, that it was bad manners.

He said, "Never leave your place with money lying around, it's an insult to the help, who are always in need of money."

I thought about that and had to agree with him.

He also sent me to Weatherall's for a fine new made-to-measure striped suit—yes, striped, and I still have it, and I can still get into it, although I am working toward being able to be comfortable in it again.

In those days I was slim, all nerve and muscle, comedy and laughter, hungry and horny. I read a story years later by Guy de Maupassant in which it was said of the central character that upon being introduced to a woman, he was ready to make love to her. (But what else? That was how I would have responded had I read that story in 1939.)

And in my new-found wealth and confidence I presumed

that if any woman I had met at a party phoned, and if she accepted my invitation to come up to 2204 at the Hampshire House, that she understood precisely why I had invited her.

And so one evening along came this skinny woman of indeterminate years who had to be at least forty to my thirty, and she is hoity-toity English, with that crazy way of talking, and like as not with a nose that really might now and then have been touched with a crushed Kleenex, and knew everybody who was anybody, or everybody who was *ever* anybody, into which category she herself apparently properly belonged, for although I knew the famous name (which I am not going to mention), it was famous not so much in connection with herself as with a number of other members of that extensive family.

Well, after listening to a lot of meaningless talk about art, and having had a few drinks, I thought the time had come to settle down to life, but this preposterous skinny broad kept running coyly about suite 2204 at the Hampshire House, until finally I opened the door and ran her out.

I never heard the end of it.

I had tried to rape her, she told the gossip columnists.

Alfonso? Who's Alfonso?

THERE ARE SOME people you can't hate, some you can't love, some you can't love or hate, but go from one to the other for an instant or two, loving and not loving, hating and not hating, and finally there are some people you can't *remember*.

There was a rather handsome lady of forty-four or more when I was twenty-six and just published and a little insane all the time from the simple joy of it, and this lady had something like hot pants for me, even though I was kind of in love with her the way Nietzsche is said to have been in love with Wagner's wife. I thought the lady was elegant, and the original woman of the world, and not really to be touched for being made of light and spirit. She insisted that I join a group of her friends, some young, some old, for cocktails at a fashionable hotel, where the lady was so well known that she was almost honored by every member of the staff.

She introduced me to each person very carefully, and she and I and a balding man of about fifty and a handsome woman of surely seventy sat at one of three tables, although her friends at the other two tables remained somewhat in our group. We talked from table to table, at any rate.

And this glorious lady began to tell me, and us, about her

adventures with Alfonso, in Canada, in Alaska, over to Greenland, and down to Manhattan.

The adventures were of a rather spicy nature, as the saying is, with the leading man Alfonso continuously superior to all other males. I tried to think who in the world Alfonso might be. Surely she didn't mean the former king of Spain, who *had* been dashing at polo, and in the salons of Europe, and at Monte Carlo gambling and dancing all night.

There was much shouting back and forth between the people at the three tables, and laughter, and drinking, and munching at niblets and neblets.

I was feeling good when once again the elegant and adored lady said, "And then we decided it was time to leave New York and get to Mexico, and in less than three minutes, Alfonso came out of a phone booth and said, 'Come on, the airplane's waiting, and we'll be in Mexico City in less than eight hours.'"

So I said, "Who *is* this preposterous wonder-worker Alfonso you keep talking about?"

Whereupon the bald-headed man said, "I am."

"But she said you're her husband, and in the stories you don't sound like a husband."

But he was, and for all I know he still is, God willing. God willing, that is, that they are both still alive. He was one of those nice people you meet and forget instantly and forever, except if you happen to ask after him, as I did, whereupon the faux pas renders him unforgettable.

I rather like people that can't be remembered, that can't really be *seen*, because they seem to be possessed of that largeness of insignificance which finally must be identified as the best order of courtesy to which man may aspire, and I am forever vigilant about a kind of courtesy I in turn owe them, and therefore I try my best not to let them go unnoticed. I fix their names on pieces of paper, and look at their faces carefully, and insist that I am going to remember them forever, but again they are instantly forgotten.

Alfonso, except for your bald head I still haven't the faintest idea who you are, and except for your always elegant wife whom I once considered a goddess, I would have forgotten you totally—and with terrible regret, although I still sometimes ask heaven itself, thinking of your wife's bragging, Who is this Alfonso, please?

Poet Larsen of *O City Cities*

WRITERS ARE a fascinating breed, because there are so many kinds of them, they are made by so many circumstances, conditions, and mysteries, and there are so many ways for writing to be done.

I remember going across the bay to Berkeley one day with a San Francisco writer named Abbott Waterbury to call on a poet friend of his. Waterbury had an editorial job on a weekly paper left over from the days of Mark Twain and Ambrose Bierce. Was it called *The Wasp?* I can't remember, and indeed I have invented the name Abbott Waterbury, since I have forgotten the fellow's actual name.

He said he had been visited in his office one day by this fellow who put down on his desk three volumes of verse and asked that as long as Abbott Waterbury was in the business of editing a literary weekly, he might as well read and review some writing that *was* writing. The editor, having reviewed my first book and having joined me several times in grappa fizzes and French fries at Izzy Gomez's Pacific Street second-floor saloon, said one evening, "Tomorrow around two I am going over to Berkeley to visit this poet, why don't you go with me?"

I picked up the editor at his office, we walked four blocks down lower Market Street, and paid a dime apiece to take the ferry across the bay. The Bay Bridge had been just lately started and wouldn't be ready for a couple of years.

On the other side, after having had coffee and doughnuts on the boat, we took a streetcar to near the University of California, walked another four blocks and went up four flights of stairs at a kind of students' dormitory, found a door, knocked, and a feeble voice asked us in.

Well, he was a frail fellow by the name of Larsen, lying on a sofa, unable to get up, even. One of his books bore the title *O City Cities*, or something like that. But the unforgettable thing was the poor fellow's lack of fire. He just had no fire, and if a writer has got to have one thing, it is a blaze going in himself, night and day. Larsen's blaze was out, and the pilot light itself was either very feeble or also out. I was puzzled, and I stood around waiting for him to respond in a reasonable manner to the arrival of visitors, not unexpected visitors, but visitors he had urged to call on him.

I watched and listened to the two of them trying to chat as if everything were just fine, Abbott Waterbury with his huge head, all disproportionate, making him look like those clowns in circuses who walk around the playing rings with enormous papier-mâché heads over their own heads, each papier-mâché made out to resemble Abraham Lincoln, Charles Lindbergh, Clark Gable, or simply Uncle Sam. Abbott Waterbury speaking with sympathy and courtesy in a discreet and soft voice, saying such things as, "Thanks for your letter about my review, I'm sorry I got so many details wrong, but I did my best."

And the poet, Larsen, not stirring at all but saying in reply something along the lines of, "Well, poetry has got to be reviewed as *poetry*, or there is no sense to it at all." Meaning as far as I was concerned nothing at all.

I was glad that even the big-headed editor had to leave the poet after less than half an hour.

Since then, however, I have looked into Larsen's book, for he did let me have a copy of *O City Cities*—did I buy it, or offer to, or what?—inscribed, and I liked the stuff, but never saw him again and have no idea what happened to him.

Runaways Walter Winchell and Robinson Jeffers

ONE NIGHT IN 1935 I came out of the Cub Room of the Stork Club in New York and found Walter Winchell standing beside the door chatting with Sherman Billingsley. Somebody introduced me to them, and without thinking, without weighing words and the effects of them, but with sincerity and warmth and even a touch of admiration, I blurted out, as I studied his sharp face with its swift and sharp eyes, "So you're Walter Winchell?"

And immediately I knew I had said the wrong thing, or at any rate that he had taken the remark as a reproof, as a belittlement, as if I had said, "So you're this guy who makes all the noise, well, Buster Boy, you aren't much, I'm a lot more than you'll ever be."

Now, of course, there was a bit of brashness in my manner as a young man, only recently sprung out of anonymity into rather large fame, certainly large enough for all practical purposes but also certainly not too large for a little kidding around.

Walter Winchell shut himself off from me instantly.

He did it with his eyes, in shock, in annoyance, in anger, and possibly even in fear.

I was not to see anything like it until several years later when I was invited to a dinner party at the hilltop estate near Los Gatos of Colonel Charles Erskine Scott Wood, author of *Heavenly Discourse*. Who had invited me to the dinner party I don't know to this day, but it was apparently for writers only, including Robinson Jeffers and his wife Una, and William Rose Benét who was just out from New York, and a few others.

In any event, I was introduced to Robinson Jeffers, who instantly turned and fled—not literally of course, only in the eyes, which made me remember my first meeting with Walter Winchell in New York.

I had long known that there was something about me that was either violent or frightening for some reason. In certain three-sided clothing store mirrors, I had for some years come upon the reflected triple images of myself with shock and disbelief, regret and shame, disappointment and despair, for I was indeed clearly violent, mad, and ugly, all because of something in me that had always been there—an intensity of some kind, a tension, an obsession with getting everything that was there to be got, a passion, an insanity, whatever might be the proper word or series of words for it.

And for hours after such an assault out of the three-sided mirror upon my illusion about myself, about my appearance, about my nature, my reality, which I wanted to believe was kindly, courteous, thoughtful, and handsome, I would be in despair about this revelation, this truth, and I would try to imagine how I might cast out the demon that was in me, or at the very least how I might keep it quiet and not so terribly noticeable.

I also felt that I must remind myself always when out among people to watch it, don't frighten people, don't go at them so intensely, keep everything cool and soft-spoken and casual, and especially watch it in meeting children, or even in looking at them in passing, for I had noticed that many little kids responded to a glance from me by bursting into tears, or turning away.

But then again there were times when kids would take to me instantly. And I had at least *that* to comfort me a little. How did it happen that those kids liked me?

The next time I ran into Walter Winchell I was more acceptable in speech and manner, and little by little we became friends.

I liked him in spite of his belief that he had enormous national and world importance, which for quite a few years, especially at the beginning of American participation in World War II, was almost justified. In his column and in his radio broadcasts, he certainly served Roosevelt's government well, as if he were a soldier carrying out orders.

He was excited about all sorts of things, all of them either spurious or inferior, but he himself had something authentic going for him all the time. It was a kind of nervous tension that pushed him, that made him dance, which I suspect is in most people who become legendary, for good or bad.

Rouben Mamoulian
Directing Miriam Hopkins
in *Becky Sharp* for Me

ROUBEN MAMOULIAN WAS a director of both stage plays and movies. He was tall and dark and slim and spoke with just enough of an accent to be exactly right for the late 1920s and all of the 1930s. He was directing one of the first all-color, all-sound, all-talking movies and I was on the set trying not to be in the way or too conspicuous, for the whole thing was out of this world, and what world could possibly be more improbable than the actual working movie-set world of the famous novel by Thackeray called *Vanity Fair*, for purposes of commerce forgotten in favor of the name of its beautiful heroine, Becky Sharp?

Even the people in the thing had this large improbable aura of other-worldliness, especially one little bit of a saucy thing named Miriam Hopkins, and all of a sudden there she was, apparently absolutely excited to be speaking to me, all about my first book, speaking in the breathless way that goes with a beautiful woman's excitement and secret language that says or seems to say, Well, now, I think I love you, I really believe I like you, and by that I don't mean talk-love, talk-like, I mean let's-get-into-bed-love.

I tried not to let my face or voice reveal or suggest what I was interpreting her face and voice to mean, for I preferred to be backward about such interpretations than to be mistaken, dead wrong, and consequently the laughingstock of myself, my soul, my very severe constant companion, guardian, critic, friend, and in nine cases out of ten my deliverer from evil, humiliation, disaster, pain, and death itself.

And so all aflame with excitement and potentialities and probable misinterpretations and definite embarrassments I tried both not to be unresponsive to the charms of Miriam Hopkins, and to cool it, not to make a public fool of myself, on the set of the world-famous director Rouben Mamoulian himself, with his own two very real names, his own two very real dark eyes behind his own very big round glasses, and his own smiling and chuckling speech with me, for he also was an Armenian, and one Armenian is very much concerned in the presence of another, the guest of another, not to embarrass the other in any way.

And so, Mrs. Beatrice Fairfax of *World Lost and Time Gone*, my problem was that I wanted to grab that little lovely thing right there and flip her over while she giggled and pretended to struggle. I wanted to let her know how really deeply she had moved me, how sweetly the phantom of the opera and the secret of the song of the soul in the opera had gathered themselves together into her bright, light, tiny, and bubbling body, which was actually telling me by word and sound and eye and scent and every other form of communication that she was mine to have and hold. And there I was anxious not to throw any kind of monkey-wrench into the machinery of the shooting of the next scene by the great movie director, my own country-man and friend Rouben Mamoulian, so of course I was very proud that when he did gently indicate to the saucy little actress that all was in readiness she instantly broke away and went to her mark and began to do precisely what she had been doing exclusively for me, now for Rouben Mamoulian, for the camera, for the world, for one person at a time in thousands of movie theatres all over the world, she began to offer herself to everybody for instant acceptance and love. And it was unmistakably clear that nobody was going to think of questioning the validity or sincerity of her offer, everybody was going to instantly love her, and at the same time I was taking great pride, Mrs. Beatrice Fairfax, in my civilized and controlled response to her exciting if terrible offer, terrible because the temptation to accept it *instantly*, was not easy to resist.

That was my problem back there in 1936 or thereabouts, Lady Beatrice, but two days later her secretary telephoned and she got on the line to chat as she had on the movie set and said with her own dear mouth not tonight but very soon she wanted me to visit her at home and have some martinis and dinner and talk and talk and talk.

After hanging up, I heard my old self say, *Talk*, did she say?

Aquitania Passengers
to Europe

THERE ARE PEOPLE we meet once, generally in travel, and find unforgettable for their humor, or ignorance, or innocence, and one of these people was a small young man on the *Aquitania* sailing from New York to Southampton in May of 1935, coxswain on the Harvard rowing team of that year. He was cheerful all the way across the Atlantic, and that made him unforgettable.

We were traveling third class, which all the same I considered luxury of the highest order. It was my first trans-Atlantic crossing, and certainly the highest shipboard luxury I had ever experienced, for I had once taken a coastwise ship from San Francisco to Los Angeles at a cost of something like eight dollars, and conditions on that little tub had been very bad, but then that had been my own fault: I hadn't enquired at all about the accommodations and food and all of the other things involved in about forty-eight hours of coastwise travel. The ship smelled like fermenting slop, the food was bad if not unwholesome, and the bunks had unlaundered linen and blankets. The other passengers were on board also because the fare was the lowest available. There were a dozen Filipino field workers up to San Francisco from the truck farms of Salinas and Monterey for a few days of recreation, whoring, drinking, restaurant-eating, shooting pool, and gambling, before going south for another season of hard work in the fields below Los Angeles.

The *Aquitania* on the other hand was enormous, one of the largest passenger ships in the world at that time, sixty thousand tons or more. And everything was clean and fresh. Although I shared a kind of arrowhead-shaped area (or room) with three other passengers, fairly well down in the bowels of the ship, I liked it and found that the upper bunk that was left for me—first come first served—was precisely the one I would have chosen had I been there first.

One of the passengers was a Serb who was going back to a village not far from Belgrade because his mother was dying, and he wanted to see her one last time, and to take her some emblems of his success in America—little gifts he was sure she would not find in her village.

He called me Mr. William, and whenever possible, whenever we happened to be in the cabin at the same time, and the other two passengers weren't there, he would continue his recitation of the story of his life, which had many sighs, head noddings, and sorrow. I didn't mind listening to this big hard-working man, for he did have real charm, and always held out a bottle of slivovitz from which he was taking nips and which he wanted me to share with him, perhaps in appreciation of my listening while I shaved or showered and got into my second suit for the evening fun and sport.

The peasant was about six feet three, about two hundred and forty pounds, a longtime worker in the steel mills of Pittsburgh, and as sensitive and courteous as a young divinity student.

His story was simple—poverty, ignorance, escape to America, hard work, pride, money, booze, jokes, women, marriage, children, time, time, time, and now he was fifty-five years old, and his mother was dying, he was no longer poor, he could afford to go and see her one last time, and he wept as he brought out the letter from his kid sister telling him, "Branco, Mama is dying, Mama is sometimes delirious, she is saying, 'Is that you Branco, my dear son?'"

And of course I felt that in listening to Branco, and in accepting nips of slivovitz I was not doing him a favor of some kind, he was doing *me* a favor—he was giving me a man's interior life without any of the literary flourishes, and every time he cried precisely like a small boy I was less saddened than gladdened, for his sorrow was beautiful, and once he looked at me while he was crying, saw my smile, and himself smiled back in a way that compelled me to burst into laughter, which in turn brought forth from him an enormous bellow of laughter, as he took three gulps from the bottle, and shouted, "Drink, drink, Mr. William, you are my friend. You understand me."

Jean Sibelius at Home
in Jaarvenpaa

I WAS BOUNCING around in a Helsingfors taxicab in July of
1935 racing north to the country house of Jean Sibelius,
the composer of *Finlandia*. I really didn't quite know what
was going on. A lot of things had happened during the
previous year, but why was I now racing forty kilometers
north to see Jean Sibelius? Was I a composer? A pianist?
A conductor? A journalist? Was I somebody who could do
him some good? Or was he somebody who could do me
some good? Or what? I really didn't want to see Jean
Sibelius or anybody else, for that matter, although I was
excited about going out there to see him, since it seemed to
be fate. I certainly had tried to stop the girl in the music
store on Annunkatu in Helsingfors from phoning Jean
Sibelius just because I had asked if I might hear *Finlandia*
in Finland, but she had refused to be stopped.

And then the great composer himself had come on the
line and had scarcely permitted me to try to identify myself
and to get out of any big deal, and at the same time to get
him out of any such deal. But he would have none of it,
and he said, "Well, you will take a taxicab, and you will
tell the driver to take you to the home of Jean Sibelius in
Jaarvenpaa. He will bring you right here."

Well, those are *instructions*, and they are from a man at
least twice the age of the writer from America, from San
Francisco, from Fresno, from Armenia, from everywhere,

from nowhere, so of course I was in no position to say, "But Mr. Sibelius, I really don't want to take up your valuable time. I just happen to have listened to *Finlandia* two or three dozen times over the past ten years, and it seemed to say something to me that was less nationalistic than private —it was music in fact that seemed to be *about* me and my particular quarrel with the world. But there's really no need for me to come out and actually see with my own eyes the man who composed that music."

I couldn't say anything.

I may be swift by nature, by character, by birth, but I am also helplessly polite, even courteous, in the most old-fashioned sense.

Besides, I was surprised by what seemed to be a boyish and boisterous courtesy on the part of a giant in the world, and not just the world of music, a giant in the world of mystery, of legend, of universal human meanings. He seemed to want me to go out there so he could see *me*, and of course he had no idea who I was.

Well, who was I?

Well, of course I was this genius, you see, whose profession happened to be writing, not composing music, who had broken into worldwide fame in no time at all, and not yet even twenty-seven years old—and the damnedest fool anybody anywhere could ever possibly see, so why not let this great man of the world see me, and compare my wild eyes and jumping nerves with his, or remember how his had been when he had been my age.

And when I say I was this genius I was hoping both to be entertaining to God and informative to the taxicab driver who had indeed, speaking excellent English, asked, "Is your profession music? Or are you in the theatre?"

Well, I *did* seem to be forever in some kind of large play whose story line was all ajumble, askew, earnest, absurd, and confusing, but I said, "No, I am not in the theatre. I am just this genius of the literary world. The California Genius of the Western World, you might say. I'm just back from Russia, you see, and it isn't heartwarming to notice that the human race under Communism is just as fraudulent as under Capitalism."

"Oh," he said, and very soon we were there.

Jean Sibelius was an enormous man with a great head, stark raving bald. He was almost as nervous as I was. He was amazed and disappointed that I didn't speak French, which he preferred to English, so he asked his young nephew just home from Stanford to interpret for him.

"Smoke this cigar," he said. "Drink this whiskey, here is my photograph, I would sign it especially to you, but my hands are shaking."

I thought, This man is a boy, his nephew is calm and collected, safely home from Stanford, but Jean Sibelius is the boy and his nephew is the old man.

I gulped down a whiskey, and tried to justify my intrusion by asking how he happened to compose *Finlandia.*

He said something that wasn't anything because the question was unanswerable, and then I said, "We hear *Valse Triste* on the radio a lot in America."

He literally groaned with pain, and I gathered that he disliked that piece, he wished to Christ he had never composed it, and I wished to Christ I hadn't mentioned it. He's got enormous works, so here's a kid from Fresno asking about *Valse Triste,* or the last moments of a fat Paris whore.

Two minutes after I had been in the house I rejoiced that I had asked the taxi driver to wait. I didn't want to take up any more of the great man's time than he himself insisted that I *must* take up.

I *had* to stay a little while, and since this was so, both for himself and for myself, I tried to make my visit reasonable, meaningful, perhaps useful *right now*, never mind the future, useful to him, and perhaps even to myself, for it was indeed myself right there in his house, was it not?

I looked around as casually as possible, and there was nobody else.

I drank a second whiskey, but refused to light one of the enormous cigars. He was smoking one as if it were a cigarette, puffing as if he might be at work on the *Elegie* of *King Christian Suite* and was determined to keep the thing inconsolable in the depth of its sorrow—not a ray of light in it anywhere, pure unadulterated despair—about death, about somebody's death, about human death, about everybody's death.

A year or two later when I first chanced upon that music on big, twelve-inch, 78-rpm phonograph records, I remembered Jean Sibelius smoking his cigar that must have cost even at that time a dollar, trying to receive an unnecessary visitor who nevertheless for some reason seemed necessary.

If he had thought that I might be somebody other than who I was, because he had not heard my name correctly, or by some other confusion, one second after he had *seen* me, he knew I was only precisely who I was, as he was only precisely who he was.

As for the Eighth Symphony the world believed he was composing at that very time and for thirty or more years thereafter, he did not ever inform anybody that there was no such symphony, that indeed he wasn't composing anything at all, that he had done his work *before* I had chanced to spend about an hour in his house and domain. He seemed to be about six feet four inches in height, two hundred and sixty pounds in weight, all of it muscle, and yet he was a very gentle, a very kind, and a very vulnerable man. He apparently could be hurt by all manner of slights, misunderstandings, discourtesies, mischief, or maliciousness. His wife, who once or twice joined the small group to see that all was well, was surely somebody who saw to it that he was not unnecessarily exposed to spiritual traumas.

Her presence reminded me not to be an awful fool in making her husband excited and unhappy about his work. Had she heard my spirited remark about *Valse Triste* perhaps? She was pretty, not quite matronly, fresh, warm, hospitable, but watchful of her man, her boy, her genius. There was laughter, and it was loud on my part, even though I myself had said the things that were intended to impel general laughter, hearty and loud on the part of the great man, while the nephew from Stanford permitted himself only a small smile. But then he was not perhaps a genius, and not nervous as the young writer was, and as the old composer was. Mrs. Sibelius laughed, apparently to inform her husband that this was nice, really, Jean, this strange noisy violent young man does admire you, he is a friend, I am glad he enjoys laughing.

The minute I got up to my room at the Torni Hotel in Helsinki around ten o'clock that night, I began to write a short story called *Finlandia*.

Two or three hours later it was done, and it appeared in my second book, called *Inhale and Exhale*.

Did I actually visit Jean Sibelius? I did.

Why didn't he do the great Eighth Symphony?

I don't know, but I wish he *had* done it, and then the greater Ninth and the still greater Tenth and Eleventh and Twelfth, because when Communism and Christianity and all of the other collective things don't do it, don't get it, the truth and sorrow of this becomes at least tolerable by means of any form of art that nervous kids of all ages all over the world find it possible and necessary to put forward.

How I Almost Met James Joyce

I NEVER MET JOYCE but I *almost* did, and I like to tell my cousins precisely how it happened.

I mean *James* Joyce of course, and this is where my cousins look at one another, and I can almost hear them asking themselves, "Is that one of the drivers for Snakey's Trucks, didn't old Snake have a driver named Jim Joyce?"

It was the early summer of the fateful year 1939, I say, and my cousins lift their shrewd eyebrows and start thinking how to get out of hearing what is clearly going to be one of the biggies, with lots of meaning. And we all knew, I go on, that the high-explosive suicidal war could no longer be stopped. Armageddon was here, the four horsemen were mounted and had their animals facing Paris itself. And so I wanted to have one last look at that famous city, and then back to New York, back to San Francisco, to wait for the draft to grab me and perhaps have me trampled to death by the terrified horses.

"Who do you like in the seventh at Bay Meadows?" my cousin Khatch said. "I mean as long as you're talking about horses."

Gourk said, "So you were in Europe, were you, at the time of the Calgary Stampede, and you met this streetwalker, is that what you would have us understand?"

And to be perfectly honest, I went on, somewhat ignoring the interruptions, except by a glance first at Khatch and another at his kid brother Gourk, there was a deep and ever-deepening pity for the poor people of the world in my heart, and everybody I came upon who looked to be likely with luck to live at least another twenty years saddened my soul in a way that was almost personal, for I knew one out of every ten would be killed in the debacle, three would be injured, and all would be given the world business of dislocation, food shortage, shelter destruction, separation from loved ones, financial bankruptcy, toothache, disgust with the government, astonishment at the attitude of the United States, and not a very nice feeling about the Pope—what did he care? He had his privacy and excellent food johnny-on-the-spot three times a day, and if necessary four.

I wandered around the streets of Paris one Saturday afternoon looking at the magnificent buildings that would soon be abandoned by the proper French government driven into hiding or exile by the enemy, contemptuously referred to as Corporal Schicklgruber but loathed and feared as Hitler, the champion monster of the Western World. If anybody could bring about the Decline of the West, as predicted by Oswald Spengler in his famous book, it was this silly-looking man who moved around like a wound-up tin toy and yet compelled the whole German nation to scream hysterically wherever he went.

"Great, great, Willie," my cousin Khatch said, "I swear to God nobody can tell an exciting story like you can."

And all of a sudden, I went on, I found myself in a bookstore, because it was called Shakespeare & Company, and I wanted to see who could possibly have thought up giving a bookshop on the Rue Odéon on the Left Bank of Paris such a name.

Well, it was a girl who immediately called up James Joyce and handed me the phone.

I said, "Mr. Joyce, I'm in town and I'd like very much to come by and say hello."

Joyce said, "Yes, well, how about Wednesday at four?"

I said, "Yes sir," even though I wanted to say, "I'm flying out tonight," but I thought I had already unwittingly and innocently intruded enough.

And that's how it happened.

I flew out that night, to London, and so I never met James Joyce.

But a few days later in Dublin I met Frank O'Connor, Sean O'Faolain, Niall Montgomery, and Brian O'Nolan, also known as Flann O'Brian, also Myles na Gopaleen.

"Gee," Gourk said. "Who else did you almost meet?"

Abandoned Bride
at the Fern Hotel

THE NIGHT BEFORE I was to take an airplane to Hollywood, to take a job at three hundred dollars a week with the B. P. Schulberg unit attached to Paramount Pictures, I wandered the streets of San Francisco, thinking. The time was October 1936, and I was twenty-eight years old. On Larkin Street I came to a narrow short street called Fern, and to a door marked Fern Hotel.

I went straight upstairs. The lady smiled pleasantly, a woman of fifty or so, large and still pretty. After I had been escorted to a little parlor, a girl came in, and I liked her so much that I didn't wait to see the other girls but went with her to the usual surreal room and removed her clothes and my own.

Afterwards, I expected her to quickly run along to other business, and when she didn't, I asked about that, and she said things were quiet, it was all right, and so we talked. She was from a family in the Midwest, father Polish, mother Lithuanian. She had such simplicity and beauty of mind that I forgot the circumstances and thought of her as a rare and delightful companion.

I asked if she could fetch a bottle, which she did instantly, and we began to drink and talk. We made love again, smoked cigarettes, drank whiskey, laughed and talked, and I told her I was flying to Hollywood tomorrow afternoon and wouldn't it be great if she would go with me?

Well, this was a mistake.

She said that she had just started, it was only a week, she had had almost nobody before me, she had never been cut to prevent conception, she could have children, she was really a good girl, as good as any virgin. I poured whiskey and lighted cigarettes and we drank and inhaled and talked and listened, and I said, "Okay, I'll come by in a taxi at two o'clock and pick you up. We'll fly there together, we'll see how it goes."

She looked at me in total nakedness, not of body alone, but also of soul, saying in her look, For God's sake, will you?

And then softly in her own sombre voice she said, "I'll never see you again."

I was crushed with shame, to the point of tears, which I saw in her own eyes.

We were together again, this time in silence, and the next day at two racing in the taxi to the airport alone I tried to put her out of my mind.

The Patriotic Revolutionary
Big-Money Non-Writers
of Hollywood

AT STANLEY ROSE'S BOOKSHOP on Hollywood Boulevard I met a lot of published writers, famous writers, hack writers, scenario writers, unpublished writers, and would-be writers. The would-be writers invariably said, "I do a little scribbling, too." And of course the minute I heard that remark I knew I was speaking to somebody likely to give Mark Twain a very short run for his money.

The scenario writers were always well-dressed, for they earned big money. They were devoted to their agents, as some men are to their mothers, because agents could work miracles on their behalf, and they enjoyed having such miracles worked. By himself a writer didn't stand a chance. It was all a matter of his agent.

I met quite a few agents at the bookshop, too, in particular a man named James Geller, who had written a couple of books himself, and who also represented Aldous Huxley.

Jim Geller was a keyed-up man, about ten or maybe even twenty years older than myself when he got me the modest job at Ben Schulberg's bankrupt studio—bankrupt in ideas, at any rate.

Another agent, a free lance, was Ben Medford, befriended by Stanley Rose, who was willing to have Ben Medford use his shop and his phone as his office, and whenever the man was broke loaned him a little money.

Charles Feldman, a big success on the other hand, although not a big reader, sometimes visited the shop and once asked Stanley, "Any promising new novelists?"

Stanley half-mumbled, "There's this Boston man, Nat Hawthorne."

And he handed Feldman a copy of *The Scarlet Letter*, saying, "I think there's a good movie in it, and I know just the right boy to do the adaptation."

"Why not get Nat himself?" the agent said, and Stanley replied, "He won't leave Boston."

A good friend of Stanley's whose name was indeed Nat was the author of *The Day of the Locust*, which several decades later was made into a big movie, but in those old and early days of Hollywood was considered an obscene libel of the sacred city.

Nathanael West was called Pep by John Sanford, another writer and a schoolmate, and he was called Tweedy Boy by Stanley Rose, because Nathanael West seemed addicted to suits made of that good heavy material.

He was a slim, solemn soul, who moved slowly, and was always open to the insult of a scenario-writing job at good money.

Sanford and West now and then did manage to get hired, and in the tradition of the time, they took the money and ran, ridiculed their employers for their rotten taste and dirty souls. Now and then, drinking in the back room at Musso and Frank's, I heard various writers cry figuratively and sometimes literally about selling their souls, about needing to earn a measly five hundred dollars a week at Warner Brothers writing pure shit, as they put it, instead of the great works of enduring worth they were born to write.

Stanley Rose would listen to crying scenario writers, and say, "Yeah, yeah, you hate having the money to buy the ambitious girls with, and the good clothes, and the good food and drink, so cry a little bit and go back there to-morrow and fart around for an hour or two for another hundred bucks—where I come from any man who earns a hundred dollars *a month* is a big success."

John Fante and Jo Pagano, both of them screenwriters, would stop by the shop fairly regularly, and then go to the restaurant next door for steaks or lamb chops, and good booze.

One day John Fante told the story about the writer's wife who was found by the writer half-dead from some kind of terrible sexual assault.

"For God's sake, honey," he said, "who did it?"

"Who did it?" his wife screamed. "Your fucking agent did it, that's who."

Whereupon the writer said, "What else did Eddie have to say?"

For the movie agent was indeed the party who kept the good times rolling.

But I despise agents, or at any rate the system that brings them into being, makes them rich and powerful. Also, lawyers. Also, publicity agents. Such people run the whole world, not just the movie world—all on ten percent of other people's earnings, the busy running little mothers.

Harry Cohn's Electric Chair and Katey's Outraged Husband

<hr style="border: double;">

I WENT HOME on foot from Columbia Pictures early one afternoon because I was a writer, and a writer doesn't keep the same hours as a factory worker. Harry Cohn, the owner of Columbia Pictures, had told me, "I don't give a shit what hours a writer keeps just so he turns in a good screenplay."

During the six previous weeks I had turned in half a dozen good movies to B. P. Schulberg—*Man Alive* was the name of one of them, *Daily News* another, but he hadn't wanted them, he hadn't been *able* to want them, and I had finally been fired for refusing to work on a scenario that was stupid—which B. P. Schulberg needed six more weeks to see for himself, a screenplay put over on him by one of the many writing Hungarian friends of the Hungarian director Charles Vidor, a writer whose name I can't remember, who couldn't write a complete sentence but could talk as fast as Ben Schulberg could listen.

Writer's agent Jim Geller told me it was not uncommon for a writer to stay only six weeks at one studio when his contract was on a week-to-week basis. He would get me a job at another studio, although it would have to be at the same wages, only three hundred a week, which in Hollywood even in 1936, was chicken feed.

Thus, two days after being fired by B. P. Schulberg, I

sat down in the seat of honor at lunch in the Writer's Dining Room at Columbia Pictures. At the other end sat Harry Cohn waiting for the big laugh, because when I sat down I got an electric shock that had sent many a new writer leaping to the ceiling, permitting Harry Cohn to roar with happiness, and permitting the older writers to compare the last victim's leap with their own. But I didn't leap, didn't feel outraged, or belittled, or even surprised, brought up another chair, and began to eat, while Harry Cohn tried not to marvel.

"Wasn't the electricity on?" he said.

"It was on all right," I said, "but I have a kind of electrical swiftness myself, so I knew the joke before it could compel a leap, that's all."

And so a week later early one afternoon, I walked from Columbia Pictures to the fourth-floor apartment at the Villa Carlotta. On the portable phonograph was a twelve-inch, 78-rpm record of *Elegie* from *King Christian Suite* by Jean Sibelius, a man I had only six months earlier visited at his country home in Jaarvenpaa.

I was enjoying this sombre music when she phoned and said, "I'm coming right up."

In one minute she was in the apartment, in my arms, and on the floor.

She said she had decided to sit in the lobby where she would not be noticed and wait until I came home. She had sat only an hour, how had it happened that I had gone home at only four in the afternoon?

She fixed scrambled eggs and drinks and she put on *Slaughter on Tenth Avenue* instead of *Elegie* and we had fun again, drank and ate again, and at six in the evening I said, "Well, you'd better go home now and get supper for your husband."

"Like hell," she said, and so during the next nine or ten

hours we made love, as the saying is, about a dozen times. Around four in the morning we went to sleep and a moment later, or so it seemed, at any rate, the desk clerk said on the phone, "A man is on his way up, and he didn't say who he is."

The man was her husband of course, and of course he wanted to kill the dirty dog who stole his wife. He broke down and cried instead, however, and took her home.

Years later I heard there are women who are insatiable. Her name was Katey, and she was such a woman, may she always find happiness—and perhaps learn to dash just a little tabasco in the scrambled eggs.

Death of a Father in *The Hush from Brooklyn to Gallup*

I HAD NEVER MET anybody with a number at the end of his name until sometime in the middle 1930s when I met James Laughlin IV, a young man of good bearing, tall, earnest, sensible, pleasant, polite, from a good family, sent to good schools, and aware of the choice a man has in how he behaves with superiors, equals, and inferiors.

He was both a publisher of new writing, and a writer of poems. His family, it turned out, were half of the big steel company Jones & Laughlin. Apparently his family had chosen not to object to his using his time and fortune in the founding of New Directions, which is still one of the few good publishing houses in America. The annual *New Directions Anthology* must by now be both forty-four years old and the repository of some of the most interesting American writing of the past half-century.

On our second or third meeting in San Francisco, James Laughlin let me know that every year he went to Switzerland to ski. At the height of the Depression, this struck me as being absolutely beautiful.

He believed that I was one of the good new writers of the country, and he invited me to contribute something to his next annual anthology, and for a couple of years I did that.

I sent him three small stories for the anthology one year

and never heard from him, so I wrote to enquire about the stories, and after a month or more a secretary replied that Mr. Laughlin was in Switzerland skiing, and that he himself, the secretary, had made a thorough search of the premises but could find nothing sent by me.

When I later wrote again, Mr. Laughlin himself replied that he was really very sorry, but he didn't remember the stories and they simply didn't seem to be in his office.

So of course I put aside any idea of sending him anything more, because one of the three stories haunted me. It came from an ache that is deep in the souls of working people, a story about the desperate pleading of a son of sixteen years, one of six or seven kids, to get his overworked father to try to take things easy, or he would surely soon be dead. The poor astonished father looked at the son and saw himself, and felt again the love he had long ago felt for all of his unborn kids, and knew again his helplessness to show that love, from being exhausted all the time, burned out by the work he had done to keep them all alive, and he couldn't even get up from the edge of his bed to embrace the boy, but finally did so a few days later, in the sleep that carried him away to death, embracing the son who had noticed him, and then all of them in one last (and first) embrace, sons and daughters gathered together in his arms, almost making a whole hard life worthwhile.

I just didn't want to have that little story lost forever, as it appears to be. Even so, now and then I like to believe that somebody somewhere will find the story and carefully preserve it, and I shall read it and say, Christ, I *thought* it was great, and it is, it really is.

But if it isn't, I shall say, Christ, it isn't great at all, what made me believe it was?

In January 1929 I sent Angel Flores a story when he was editor of some little magazine or other, and never got it back, but for years kept nagging at him and his associates to look for *The Hush from Brooklyn to Gallup*. And one day sure enough, after twenty-five years, Angel Flores himself found the story, insisted on keeping the original manuscript, and sent me a Xerox copy.

I read it and felt, Ah hell, it was better than this when I sent it.

Angel Flores finally sent *something*, at any rate, but James Laughlin never did.

Has there been a *real* loss? Good God, no. Good God, yes. (Take your choice.)

The Truth about the Explosion on Lower Market Street

Nobody, and that means nobody whatsoever, should be put in a penitentiary, but Mooney and Billings *were* put in a penitentiary, and for years American liberals tried to get them sprung, as *they* had tried to spare the lives of Sacco and Vanzetti, and had failed.

My sympathies invariably go to the convicted, and never to those who are unconvictible, although they are as pitiful as everybody else.

Even when trials are held and the newspapers are full of the proceedings, and the television screens receive the living story on the spot for all the world to see, and there seems to be a human effort to achieve justice, I find the whole thing a theatrical performance, astonishing, amusing, and entertaining, but always in a horrible way.

The organized clamor on behalf of Mooney and Billings was based on their illegally proven but morally unproven guilt about a death-dealing explosion during a Labor Day Parade up Market Street in San Francisco early in this century, but that to me is more of the same irrelevance of the whole justice business—they do not *need* to be innocent of anything to be sprung, they need to be understood, and having been understood, those who have understood them need then to understand themselves and to know themselves to be as guilty or as innocent as the two men in jail, or as in the case of Sacco and Vanzetti the two men deprived of life and elevated to martyrdom.

Near the time of his deliverance at last, his pardon and release, Tom Mooney spent quite a lot of time in the San Francisco Jail, on Kearny Street near Commercial, and on two or three occasions in 1935 and 1936 I visited him there, and we sat and talked, and the people who had arranged for me to visit the pale quiet old fellow expected me to write about him, to add something to the campaign to get him out of jail. And of course I did.

But Mooney himself seemed perfectly happy to be in jail.

He loved having been made a hero of the working class, and even of Communism, and he spent his days and nights in full awareness that rightly or not he was the star of a large drama and that the newspapers not only of San Francisco but of the whole country and the whole world were following his case, his story, his martyrdom, his defiance of reactionary society, or at least his indifference to that society's desire and intention to bury and forget him.

I spoke two languages with Tom Mooney, and I believe he understood them both. One language spoke to the hero and martyr, the other to the simple human being.

Now, I know I have no right to say this and will be criticized for doing so, but I believe that Tom Mooney had me understand, willfully, that he had indeed had some vital connection with the explosion on Market Street that had taken so many lives. If not, then he certainly *wished* he had, or liked to pretend that he had.

He was soon released and went off with his wife, Rena, and became a free man, and then died.

But if Tom Mooney, in God's head and eye, had no

connection with the explosion, it certainly *happened*, and the need for it to happen is the only thing to study—it is irrelevant who was connected with it.

If that doesn't satisfy the classic legal obsession for the legal and irrelevant truth, then let it be understood that I planned and executed the whole thing.

The Fight between Diego Rivera and Leon Trotsky and Josef Stalin

I WENT DOWN to Mexico City by train from San Francisco sometime in April of 1939. After crossing the border at Nogales, an old-time American on the train told me that in all his forty years in Mexico he had never carried a gun because he wanted it known to everybody that he was un-armed: he was *honest* and didn't *need* to carry a gun. In any kind of discussion with anybody, he spoke softly, and he was never tempted to be a hero, or to engage in any kind of heroics. Heroes and heroics, he suspected, were the in-ventions of writers. And so when he asked my work, I said I was a vineyardist, but the next day I decided, Ah the hell with it, and I let him know that I was a writer, short stories so far, but at that very moment a play of mine was being put on in New York, called *My Heart's in the Highlands*.

"I never knew a writer," he said, and I said, "Well, the best place to know them is in their writing, in any case."

"I read the Bible, although I'm not a religious man," he said. "I suppose it's because the Bible was read to me when I was a kid."

There was more to him than he put forward or that I was able to gather, and the thing I liked best about him was his worldly and even complicated simplicity, tempered by much hard experience. And I wondered if there were many Americans like him in Mexico, in Central America, and in

South America. Over the years it came to me that yes, there are always a great many of these special Americans everywhere, along with similar Chinese, Syrians, Jews, Indians, Irish, English, Germans, Italians, and Armenians. They *are* a special breed, if I may put it that way: without forsaking the mother-country, or culture, they are essentially themselves alone, each of them, and they need the arena of the whole world rather than the narrow limits of a single country.

Having worked on Fresno vineyards with Mexicans, and having at the same time read Carleton Beals on Mexico and the Mexicans, I had always wanted to visit Mexico, so now I was there, and it seemed to me that I had better take a taxicab out to the house of Diego Rivera.

He had been to San Francisco putting up a large mural in the Stock Exchange. Albert M. Bender, the rich patron of the arts, had spoken to me about him. Ralph Stackpole, the sculptor, had spent time with him. Matthew Barnes, the plasterer who painted the desolation of the human soul, had *watched* him work. The roly-poly Mexican artist was at the center of much cocktail-party talk and barroom shouting in San Francisco for a long time, but none of the people who had known him had written a letter of introduction for me. I just thought I would go out and say hello (a stupid thing for anybody to do, of course). I had found his name and address in the phone book and hadn't found the name and address of José Clemente Orozco, who *was* the greatest painter in Mexico. (At that time I hadn't even *heard* of Siqueiros or Tamayo, the youngest of a great lot.)

There was another reason I believed I might risk not being too much of a nuisance by taking a taxicab ride to the house of Diego Rivera—I knew he was a friend of Leon Trotsky. Perhaps Trotsky would be there, and if not, perhaps Rivera would telephone him and help me get to *his* house, too. Finally, even while riding out over the hot dusty streets of the outskirts of Mexico City to Diego Rivera's house I thought, Well, I can always just decide not to go to the gate and ring the bell.

But I did, and a servant came to the gate and went to report who was calling, whereupon the servant escorted me into the studio. I saw a short heavy man about ten years older than myself, smiling and painting. Sitting for him was his wife, a slim woman, partly German, Frida Kahlo.

I thanked him for letting me pay my respects even while he was working. It was an honor to be in his house at such a time, but of course I would be leaving in a minute. "No no no," he said, "we will have some tequila in a little while."

We talked, and his wife did not talk, perhaps in order to keep her pose, very simple, very natural, perhaps not, perhaps because it was her nature, and then I said, "And I would like to pay my respects to Leon Trotsky."

"Ah," Diego Rivera said, "had you come day before yesterday I could have arranged it, but yesterday I had a fight with Mr. Trotsky about what is best for the people of the world, and we are not speaking—I am afraid he would not want to see you if you happened to mention my name."

He was a very decent man to let me barge in on him, I'm glad I saw him in action, but I wish he hadn't had that fight, because I never did meet Trotsky, and I really wanted to. I wanted to try to figure out why he lost out to Joseph Stalin, the boyhood friend of Anastas Mikoyan and other Armenian revolutionaries. The theory was that Leon Trotsky insisted that the Revolution had to be worldwide, and that Joseph Stalin knew better. I doubt it. That's too simple. And had I met Leon Trotsky I think I would have been able to figure out why the lowbrow Georgian had out-witted the highbrow German-Jew.

Drinking tequila, Diego Rivera said, "We fight, we are always fighting, all of us revolutionaries. It is disgraceful. It is silly. It is very sad. But it is necessary. It is us. But Trotsky is a fool, too, of course."

A Little of the Immortality and a Few of the Immortals of 57th Street

I HAVE ALWAYS HAD a fondness for the south side of 57th Street in New York between Seventh Avenue and Sixth Avenue, for it is on that side that we have Carnegie Hall, saved at the last minute from demolition by a great variety of outraged citizens. And we have The Russian Tea Room, Marboro Books, The Great Northern Hotel, although it is no longer there, and the Automat, which is no longer what it used to be.

I used to stay at the Great Northern Hotel. I liked the name of the place, and the rooms were large and spacious. I wrote *The Time of Your Life* there, when the weekly rate was not much more than eighteen dollars, and just a few years earlier had been only twelve dollars.

From my room I used to duck down to the street and into the Automat for coffee and doughnuts, a nickel for the coffee, and a nickel for the two doughnuts. And now and then for three nickels a baking dish of beef pie, the nearest thing to the lost but unforgotten, unforgettable, meat pie of the Irish cook at the Fred Finch Orphanage.

But of course this visit to the Automat for food was also a visit for people. And they are never more amusing than at meals, especially in a place like the old Automat. One day a man came and sat at my table and said he had produced a social play called *One Third of a Nation*, and he had seen *My Heart's in the Highlands*, and he would like to say hello but at the same time he would be thrilled if he might produce one of my plays.

He said his name was Dudley Murphy, and of course it was.

We sat and drank coffee and talked, and I then hurried back through the narrow entrance of the Great Northern and into the elevator to the fourth floor and down the hall to room 428 and back to my work, for the hardest thing about writing a play is being willing, just being willing to keep after the thing, no matter what, and to keep it moving with people and talk and things happening. And the easiest thing about writing a play or about writing anything else is going off to eat and drink and talk to people and *not* to go back to work.

I never offered Dudley Murphy a play, but many years later when I occupied a small beach house at Malibu, I used to drive to Holiday House, a little north on the highway, and there I would be greeted by Dudley Murphy, who owned the place, and had gone into *that* side of showbiz, so to put it.

The writer Harry Roskolenko used to be a frequent visitor at the 57th Street Automat, and now and then our visits there would coincide and we would sit and talk about the old days when everybody had really believed that the new world was indeed about to begin—the days of the early 1930s. It seemed everybody was a Communist in those days, excepting me. As for Harry, he had always insisted that he was a Trotskyite.

All along 57th Street one is forever coming upon somebody who has done something somewhere in a very special way.

One day just across from the Great Northern I saw a small man who had lately lost a leg. He was standing near the highly polished brass hydrant in front of Steinway & Sons, and so I went across the street to pay my respects. It was Jimmy Savo, the little pantomime clown who could make your heart heave with sudden sorrow for the whole human race in all of its anguish and loneliness. He looked precisely the same as when he performed, and he had the same tiny sweet smile and the same puzzlement and expectation in his eyes.

He had heard my name, he said, but I knew that that wasn't why he was so pleased that I had gone over to speak to him. He had wanted somebody to do that, and anybody would do.

He talked about having gone to Italy and having bought a castle and having lived in it, and what he was saying was that it was all really wonderful but still very lonely.

That was the only time I saw him, and a year or two later I read in *The New York Times* that he had died.

The Light Fantastic
of George Jean Nathan

IT IS UNDERSTANDABLE that Henry Louis Mencken would
be pleased to have as his best friend for half a century
or more George Jean Nathan. They were altogether un-
alike, and therefore precisely suitable for friendship. A
rough-and-tumble newspaperman and an elegant dandy
drama critic, one a German, the other a Jew. The theory
persists that H. L. Mencken was anti-Semitic, but I never
saw any evidence of it either in his writing or in his
conversation.

In his contribution to a series entitled *Living Philosophies,*
first published in a national magazine, perhaps *The Bookman,* and then in a book, George Jean Nathan said that he
had no impulse at all to love the Armenians, and H. L.
Mencken wrote somewhere that any beggar who ap-
proached an Armenian for a handout was a fool and a
dreamer, because no Armenian ever gives money to beg-
gars. Even so, I never felt that either of these remarks
demonstrated that these men were anti-Armenian. And
when both of these editors ignored the young writer in
Fresno who now and then sent an essay to *The American
Mercury,* I did not feel that this was because they had
recognized the writer's name as Armenian. I presumed that
they didn't like my writing. Furthermore, had they indeed

been out-and-out anti-Armenian, I really doubt that their attitude would have cancelled out for me the rest of the character of each of them.

I had always liked the writing of the two friends, Mencken and Nathan, and so early in 1939 when I arrived in New York by Grace Line ship from Vera Cruz, and went to the Guild Theatre on 52nd Street and saw the fourth performance of my first play, *My Heart's in the Highlands*, and the next day read George Jean Nathan's review in one or another of the national weeklies, I was delighted that he liked the play.

I didn't mind at all that Burns Mantle writing for the *News* and Sidney Whipple for the *Telegram* considered the play a hoax. They were not drama critics in any case, notwithstanding that Burns Mantle appeared to be the founder and editor of the *Best Plays of the Year*, a worthy project that continues to this day.

If George Jean Nathan liked *My Heart's in the Highlands*, I didn't care who didn't like it. What's more, he voted for the play at the Drama Critics' Circle, which convened at the Algonquin Hotel, and one day out of the blue telephoned me at the Great Northern Hotel. For the first time in my life in April of 1939 I heard his elegant, slightly quavering voice. He told me that he was inviting me on behalf of the Drama Critics' Circle to the annual Awards Dinner, would I be able to make it?

Well, I was never a snappy dresser, and I went where I liked, and I probably really couldn't be counted on to behave as drama critics preferred their honored guests to behave.

Thinking of all this, I nevertheless replied, "Yes, sir, I'll be there, and I'll be neat."

I think it was this demonstration of a willingness to meet

convention halfway that made George Jean Nathan believe we ought to meet for a drink at his corner table at the famous 21 Club.

In any case, it was probably his campaigning on my behalf that got me up to the Awards Dinner, and put me across the table from Eddie Dowling, who told me that he would produce sight unseen any play I might care to write. And *that*, in turn, sent me to work the following Monday morning on the writing of *The Light Fantastic*, which George Jean Nathan read in manuscript and thought might better be called *The Sunset Sonata*, thinking somewhat of August Strindberg. In the end, however, the play was called *The Time of Your Life*. It was written in six days, by a rube who didn't know the first thing about dramaturgy, a rustic who was not in the Group Theatre, and did not consider Harold Clurman an oracle of art, the first authority of the modern American theatre, and the all-around curator of culture for the masses.

The fact is I found him bumbling in thought and speech, with a tendency to hysteria. There was a miscalculation in his mind about the connection between himself, theatre, culture, politics, women, and the human race. He loved to gather the faithful around him and to pontificate in the most indulgent manner for hours, delighting in the admiration of ambitious actors and actresses, an order of society excessively vulnerable to even spurious articulation of ideas and theories related to their problems of identity, function, and effectiveness.

The night I saw *My Heart's in the Highlands* I went on to a party that included most of the cast and a great many of Harold Clurman's friends, including his wife at that time, Miss Stella Adler. He talked continuously, and now and then almost but not quite said something. *Rubber mouth* is the way I thought of him quite spontaneously and help-lessly.

As a gesture, and indeed as a requirement of courtesy and gratitude for the fact that the Group Theatre had produced *My Heart's in the Highlands,* I offered him *The Time of Your Life,* which I felt sure he *would* accept, making it necessary for me to write another play for Eddie Dowling—which would have been just fine, too, keeping me busy at new writing in a new form, or at any rate an old form which I was now at last beginning to manage with a certain native virtuosity. (The first thing I wrote, on lined tablet paper, and then on the first typewriter I ever owned, was in fact a play.) But Harold Clurman did not even reply to my note, attached to the play. I expected him to reply in a matter of forty-eight hours at the most. After quite a long time, perhaps two weeks, he telephoned and asked me to meet him at his office. When I got there, he picked up the manuscript and said, "I'm not going to produce this play, and I want to tell you why."

"I'm not interested in why," I said. And I took the play and left his office.

He would have talked for two hours, and for all I know he might have talked himself into producing the play, after all—and ruining it forever. Or he might have made me understand that you don't just write a play, you think about it, you discuss it with your girl, with your friends, with your mother, with Harold Clurman, and then perhaps if *they* feel you are really ready, you take at least a whole year to give it a go, and then and only then you deliver the first draft. How dare you just write a play?

George Jean Nathan never had anything *instructive* to say about the *writing* of plays, but he knew more about the theatre than anybody else I have ever talked with. He passed along what he knew in a way that was easy for me to take or leave. And his talk both invited and compelled participation on my part, and on the part of anybody else who happened to be at the table.

Once it was two Chinese girls, who were actually Japanese, but on account of Pearl Harbor had to watch it: they were delightful, in any case, and so one drink became two, then eight drinks, dinner, brandy, the Cub Room, and finally around four in the morning George Jean Nathan climbed very carefully out of a taxi at the Royalton and I took the girls on to the Victoria. But when I reached the Great Northern there were six messages from one of the girls, so I went up there, because she said on the phone, "I want to know more about the source of drama."

There were many great evenings with George Jean Nathan both before and after the War, when I disappeared from Broadway for the three years I was in the Army, and for all practical purposes forever after. During my absence all sorts of hustlers with sharp agents got busy and got rich. And after the War all I had was a condition of simple madness, the consequence of having been for three years subjected to unremitting chicken. I also had a wife and a son. I also had a theory that now I would get back to the proper founding of the family, and return to my proper work stronger than ever.

I was dreaming. My major work turned out to be to keep the bride, now the mother also of a daughter, not quite so desperately unhappy, and this meant moving a lot: from San Francisco to Oyster Bay, back to San Francisco, and then to Manhattan, where one day I ran into George Jean Nathan at 21. He said, "Well, where are you, what are you up to?"

"I'm looking for an apartment," I said. "There are four of us now, you know."

"Why don't you go to Poland?" he said, and I knew one man remained in a silly world who still made sense—he *laughed*, at any rate.

And then all of a sudden he was sick, and it was terrible.

By that time I was no longer able to deceive myself into any theory of being married, of having a wife, of being involved in the bringing up of two kids. It just wasn't so. I had spent half a million dollars trying to insist that it *was* so, and that there would be more children.

I had begun to stop at the Royalton Hotel for a number of reasons, not the least of which was the lower rates, the bigger rooms, the high ceilings, the central location, and the tradition of the place. Also I had come to dislike the Algonquin, just across the street, and the everlastingly gushy crowd there. As far as I was concerned, for half a century the real writers had gone to the Royalton while the dilettantes had gone to the Algonquin. At any rate, Robert Benchley, to mention only one other besides George Jean Nathan, had lived at the Royalton.

I liked it there, and I began slowly to get back to work. Three years in the Army and a stupid marriage had all but knocked me out of the picture, and, if the truth is told, out of life itself.

But now it was George Jean Nathan who was in terminal illness during one of my prolonged visits at the Royalton.

Julie Hayden, who had become his wife, telephoned now and then to let me know the situation, and I would drop by and find the magnificent fellow in a robe, almost totally nullified by illness, sitting in virtual darkness listening to a Catholic priest. He became a convert and quite a few people were shocked, as if at the last minute he had let them down.

To me his conversion seemed altogether personal and therefore beyond my understanding, and none of my business, precisely as T. S. Eliot's had been. You live and die according to what goes on in yourself, which no one else can even begin to know, not even father, mother, wife, son, or daughter.

One evening the phone rang and his voice from just two floors below and midway down the hall, directly across from the elevators, was young and alive, and he said, "Not tonight, but this coming Saturday, let's get out on the town, keep Saturday open, I'll call you." Oh boy, I thought. He can't move, he has to be helped out of bed to get to a chair at the card table where he sits to chat softly with the priest for hours, so we're going out on the town Saturday night. And of course there would be no call at all on Saturday. A week or two later he would phone again and say pretty much the same thing.

Brooks Atkinson visited him faithfully for surely longer than a year. And there were others, but not many.

And then he died, and Broadway was diminished enough not to be thought of seriously again.

Did he really do anything for Broadway, for New York, for America, for the theatre, for art, for life?

Yes, he did. He dressed neatly and he went out among the thieves and assassins. And in his quavering voice he greeted beautiful girls and berated and scorned frauds of all categories. And he wrote. He was always writing. And everything he wrote had laughter in it. He was one of the most serious men in the living world, certainly as serious as his old friend, H. L. Mencken, but he refused to burden his writing, or his readers, with the agony of his unconverted and apparently indestructible soul. And then it *was* destructible, and being held fast to one small place, a small suite at the Royalton, he didn't know what to do, what to do. There can't ever be anybody like him again.

Love's Old Sweet Song
and *The Grapes of Wrath*

WALTER HUSTON OPENED in a play entitled *A Passenger to Bali*, directed by his son John, which I went to see at the urging of Lawrence Langner of the Theatre Guild. Langner believed the play would fail, and that perhaps Walter Huston would then accept the part of Barnaby Gaul in my play *Love's Old Sweet Song*.

I thought *A Passenger to Bali* was just fine. Walter Huston's performance was excellent, and John Huston's staging of the play was just about perfect.

"So," I said to Langner, "what makes you think the play isn't going to be a success?"

He was a lawyer, specializing in patents, a man of perhaps fifty in 1940 to my thirty-one, and I rather thought of him as having no real right or reason to be associated in any activity related to the theatre beyond bookkeeping and finances, but he imagined himself to be in the creative end of the business, and spoke proudly of his visits with George Bernard Shaw, several of whose plays Langner and his closest associate Teresa Helburn had produced for the Theatre Guild. Langner had even written a play that had actually been produced. He said it was a bedroom farce. This made me look at him twice, for he just wasn't the boy for *any* kind of farce writing, let alone bedroom.

We found our way backstage after the opening-night

curtain calls, which had numbered not more than five or six, and Langner pointed out that in a big hit the audience sometimes doesn't let the curtain come down and stay down for a full half-hour—applauding becomes a kind of compulsion, and people stand up but refuse to leave the theatre.

In short, a kind of hysteria takes place, altogether embarrassing to anybody not childish, and unacceptable to any real playwright.

The curtain calls at *A Passenger to Bali* had used up no more than a minute. And indeed there was a sober quietude in Walter Huston's dressing room. His son was there, quietly puffing on a small cigar the precise shape of a cigarette.

I considered our arrival an intrusion and wanted to leave after saying that I really liked the play very much, which was the truth.

Walter Huston thanked me, wiped the makeup from his face, got into a shirt, and said to his son, "Well, let's just not *expect* good reviews, but let's also just wait and see."

We walked with him to the street and said so long, whereupon Langner said, "He'll do Barnaby Gaul."

"How do you know?"

"It'll take some talking and some juggling of the money, but he'll do it. *A Passenger to Bali* won't run a week."

Langner turned out to be right, and so I directed Walter Huston in *Love's Old Sweet Song*, one of my favorite plays. It failed, however, even after we had all worked very hard in Philadelphia, and then in Baltimore. Some people said the Okie family in the play was meant to belittle John Steinbeck's people in *The Grapes of Wrath*. No such thing.

A few years later I was crossing Van Ness Avenue at Tulare Street in Fresno when Walter Huston drove up in an open car. He stopped and called out to me. With him were friends from Hollywood visiting his orange grove near Porterville.

"This is Bill Saroyan," he said. "Best damned director I ever worked with."

Well, we *had* worked together, and we had had fun, so perhaps I was not too big a fool in being pleased by his kind words.

One of the Great Mothers
of the World

THERE ARE many mothers in the world, and every man runs into his share of them. L. B. Mayer, who pretty much owned and operated what I used to call the Laundry, Metro-Goldwyn-Mayer, when that place was in its prime, is one of the great mothers of all time.

He had a potbelly and a direct line to the current President, from Calvin Coolidge to Franklin Delano Roosevelt. And he even stayed in touch with the candidates who lost, such as Alf Landon and Wendell Willkie.

What for? Well, he had stars, like Clark Gable and Carole Lombard, for instance, and they could always be useful to the government when it had a piece of political propaganda to put over on the people.

L. B. Mayer had a good thick face with a kind of round quality to it and a sharp nose. And he had a reputation that was enormous, and evil.

All of his slaveys, especially in the writing department, told stories about him every day, and pretty much every night. He could make or break movie people, in all departments, and he did so whenever desirable or necessary. He was faithful to the faithful and ruthless with the smart alecks, as he put it. Anybody who got sarcastic with old L. B., even only in the eyes, giving him only a sarcastic *look*, would soon enough learn that L. B. would take it slow and easy, and then at an unexpected moment take his revenge. Like death itself.

When L. B. Mayer wanted to con me about movie rights to *The Human Comedy*, he called in Eddie Mannix, Sam Katz, Benny Thau, and the best man of the lot, Bernie Hyman. These men gave him moral and legal support, and he gave them another lesson in motherhood.

Eddie Mannix arrived with a big smile on his face. Sam Katz came less cheerfully, more warily. He was physically a much smaller man than Mannix and apparently much more aware of the realities of power maneuvering among the top half dozen executives at M.G.M. They were all at work for the company and the owners, a certain Mr. Nick Schenk, and a certain Mr. Lowe, who was never referred to by his first name. But they were also at work for number one, as they liked to put it in private.

Benny Thau was a slim swift lawyer who was there primarily to keep L. B. Mayer informed about the legalities or illegalities of any given situation, and to draw up an agreement on the spot.

"This is the best agreement I have ever handed to anybody," L. B. Mayer said to me, looking at Benny Thau. "I want the very best deal for this boy who has written this amazing story about life in wartime America. Lillian Messenger read the story to me while I sat at this very desk three weeks ago and listened to every word she read for almost two hours, and I cried—yes, gentlemen, tears poured out of my eyes, and I want this boy to have our very best contract, do you understand, Mr. Thau?"

And of course Mr. Thau understood perfectly. Not so, my agent, however. He wasn't even there.

There were several reasons why Stanley Rose was my agent. In the first place, he had informed me while I was rolling dice in Las Vegas that he could get me a job at

M.G.M. for big weekly money in case I wanted a job. In the second place, he was bankrupt, owing to the fact that almost all of his Hollywood customers owed him great sums of money but refused to pay, or paid only in very small installments. His bookshop was in danger of being closed. He said that if he could get ten thousand dollars soon, he could save the shop.

Well, *somebody* had to be the agent in any case, why not Stanley Rose?

But he was deliberately kept out of these earliest meetings. Vic Orsatti, L. B. Mayer's *private* agent, as it were, poured good whiskey for Stanley Rose on his daily arrival at the studio, and kept him pleasant company, far from where business was being transacted.

But when things began to be super-clever, and the bullshit was flying fast, and L. B. Mayer was performing the part of the great benefactor of American writing, I said, "Shouldn't my agent be here?"

L. B. Mayer got to his feet, almost in a rage: "Why isn't this boy's agent here?" he said. "Who is responsible for this?"

His associates didn't even look at one another, for they *knew* who was responsible. Thereupon, the guilty party said, "All right, all right, Mr. Thau, go out and find this boy's agent. Who is he? William Morris? Charles Feldman? Irving Lazar? Vic Orsatti?"

The rhetorical question permitted me to remark, "My agent is Stanley Rose."

L. B. Mayer pretended to be confused.

"But isn't he a *bookseller?* Don't I see him going down the hall of the Writers' Building carrying a satchel of books every now and then? How could *he* be your agent?"

Even so, Stanley Rose was quickly brought into the meeting in L. B. Mayer's enormous private office. Stanley tried his best to keep his equilibrium, and L. B. Mayer said, "Mr. Rose, I want this boy here who has written this patriotic story of simple Americans in a simple American town living simple American lives to have the best deal that I have ever given any writer. And I want this deal to have his approval, and the approval of his agent. He tells me *you're* his agent. Is that true?"

"Yes, sir, I am his agent," Stanley Rose said, "and I want him to have the best deal, too. What *is* the deal?"

Everybody then looked at one another, for hardly were the words out of his mouth than Stanley Rose shut his eyes and appeared to be fast asleep.

L. B. Mayer spoke almost directly to Eddie Mannix.

"Let's have some coffee, gentlemen."

Eddie Mannix got to his feet.

"What's coffee got to do with the deal?" Stanley Rose said. He also got to his feet.

Soon we were all standing around, sipping coffee and talking, and believing in America, the home of mothers, and the hope of fathers.

Stanley Rose got his ten thousand dollars, kept his shop open, and visited his mother Kate in Matador, Texas.

I got cheated, but legally, the motherly way.

L. B. Mayer died, and everybody who was anybody loved his funeral.

A Moment of Mack Sennett, Another of D. W. Griffith

I'M REMEMBERING PEOPLE the way all of us remember them, without order or system.

As memory brings them around I remember them in a little writing, I don't try to portray them in anything like the fullness and depth of the portrait painter, or in anything like the meaning one might expect of a character in a work of fiction. I only remember them, and they are only *myself* remembering them, they are not themselves remembering themselves.

Who are people to me other than what I knew of them? And other than what I myself was at the time?

The early world of Hollywood, which at the time did not seem early at all, was the world that belonged somewhat to D. W. Griffith at one end, and somewhat to Mack Sennett at the other. Top and bottom, so to say. Head and tail.

At Stanley Rose's bookshop I met Mack Sennett one day, and he told me about his career as a maker of the Keystone Cop comedies, with the pretty girls in the old-fashioned bathing suits, including Gloria Swanson, who in 1976 is still going strong. Very old-fashioned herself, very much opposed to the nudity in so many of the new movies, and still with the famous smile and face and teeth, and whatever else constitutes the Gloria Swanson identity—a kind of porcelain quality of face.

Mack Sennett was a man of medium height, a little on the thick side, and the day I met him, not at all lively in speech, mind, eye, or gesture, totally unlike his lunatic comedies. As a matter of fact, he was a little depressed, as men are when their day is done but they themselves are still up and about. He did not seem to *really* know anything at all about the comic *art* aspect of his product. That sort of fancification had come from various early fans, like Gilbert Seldes, who were writing for magazines like *Vanity Fair*. Mack Sennett was only a workingman who had fallen into the making of movies, first up at Niles, he said, not far from San Jose, where Bronco Anderson had made two or three dozen two-reel westerns, straight from Brooklyn.

Mack Sennett may have been many things to many people. He was certainly an embracing mother to many pretty girls, but now he was an old man going to the free places in town, to kill a little time.

D. W. Griffith on the other hand, at least according to another frequent visitor at the Stanley Rose bookstore, Seymour Stern, was the greatest man of all time in the world of movies. We met in the ticket line at the 55th Street Theatre in New York just off Seventh Avenue: *Potemkin*, I think the movie was. We had an earnest little chat.

He was tall, courtly, soft-spoken, and also finished.

But what's wrong with being finished? You go to a bookshop and hang around, no charge. You stand in line at an art movie and chat with fellow line-standers, one dollar admission.

Being finished has its place, it's certainly peaceful, and it can't be beat for becoming really real at last.

Life, Art, Politics, and Lunch at Hyde Park

THE LUNCHEON TOOK PLACE in the garden of the President's summer residence at Hyde Park. I'm not sure the tables were assigned, but I found myself at a table for four just to the left of where Franklin Delano Roosevelt was to sit, at the head of a very long table, at which already were seated Hendrik Willem van Loon, a writer of popular history, and F.P.A., or Franklin P. Adams, a man who for a hundred and eighty-four years had been getting out a daily newspaper column entitled *The Conning Tower* (or at any rate something like that), to which a wide (but not really terribly wide) variety of people had been sending little tidbits of writing in both doggerel and straight language. And gathered around this main table were dozens of men and women waiting for the arrival of the President, who was to greet the people of the arts, the writers, the newspaper columnists, the actors, the actresses, and similar fish easily schooled into a net. It was the eve of the campaign for an unprecedented third term, and the President and his people were determined not to lose the election.

On the other hand, the upstart Wendell Willkie seemed determined to keep the great aristocrat of American democracy from breaking with tradition. Wendell Willkie had recently returned from a nonhazardous trip around the world, and had come out with a small book aptly entitled *One World*, and he seemed to be swiftly winning the affection and respect of the voting people.

Hence, this lunch at Hyde Park: stop Willkie. Invite writers to lunch, and stop him cold. And of course a President *can* round up very nearly anybody he likes.

My invitation was both unaccountable and informal, if not irregular. I received nothing in the mail. Nobody phoned. Nobody, that is, except the playwright Sidney Kingsley, who called from somewhere in New Jersey to say that he and his wife Madge Evans were driving to Manhattan tomorrow, Sunday, and then they were going on to Hyde Park, for lunch with the Roosevelts, how about going with them?

I seem to have an insatiable curiosity, and I certainly like rides out of Manhattan into the country, so I said, "Sure, I'll be ready."

Madge Evans drove, and years later, she and Sidney Kingsley at Leonard and Sylvia Lyons' one night asked if I remembered how our car was stopped for speeding and how I argued with the cop—and won, or was it that I had argued in vain?

In any event, I forgot all about *that* episode, although I did not forget about being put down by Miss Katharine Hepburn for opening my big mouth about her participation in a political program that everybody seemed to believe would improve everything everywhere instantly. She was carrying under her arm a stationery box, the contents of which rattled as she bounded about, and so I was unable not to ask, "Are they in that box, Miss Hepburn—all the answers?"

The elegant lady gave me a very icy look and said, "It's none of your business what's in the box, Mr. Saroyan."

That was a very nice reply, with flawless diction and timing, as if in a Philip Barry play, perfectly spoken and timed.

And I don't consider it odd that in the intervening years I have come to take pride in not having said anything more, for whatever *had* been in the box, it very probably hadn't been answers.

The President was lugged in by two secret service men and placed in his chair at the head of the long table, and everybody quickly sat down, because he had other plans for the afternoon. He wanted to get his part in this New England chowder lunch with the arty crowd over with as soon as possible, so that Eleanor could carry on in her usual thorough and efficient manner, while his elegant mother, Mrs. James Roosevelt, observed Eleanor, and now and then chatted with a guest: "Does Franklin seem a little tired to you, Mr. Saroyan? He does, to me."

So there I sat, and across the table for four was James Thurber, and beside him sat his wife.

After lunch, I said to James Thurber that I would not be going up to shake the hand of the President, as everybody else was doing. James Thurber also declined to honor, or to bother, the President, or himself.

Thus, only a political anarchist, who voted once at the age of twenty-one and never again; and a humorous writer and cartoonist, who could no longer see—only these two, unrelated and unrelatable, did not that fine Sunday afternoon, shake the hand of Franklin Delano Roosevelt.

Sensible and Stupid
about Blackmail
at the Knickerbocker Hotel

I was at the Knickerbocker Hotel, and across the street at the Knickerbocker Tailors I was having four suits and two overcoats made to order, from being rich.

I would ask up to my rooms whoever I knew was in town whom I had known over the years, and they would come up and we'd order drinks and little sausages wrapped in bacon and held together by toothpicks, and other junk, and we would drink and eat and tell jokes and laugh. I was spending money. I wasn't spending anywhere near enough, though, because all of a sudden money had begun to rush in upon me, and I was using it mostly for sensible, family things. I was not banking a dollar of it. I was getting rid of it, because there was plenty more where that came from.

The year was 1941, the month October, the world was going through awful traumas of many kinds, and all I was doing was looking for tail.

Just down the hall at the Knickerbocker Hotel was a voluptuous woman of about forty-four, absolutely stacked, who had come to Hollywood to get her daughter into films.

When they came out of the elevator together as I was waiting to get in, they were absolutely dazzling and intoxicating, and they gave off a blossomy, bosomy scent that gave me an instant hard-on. They were a couple of gorgeous flowers of the sweetest botanical order.

I watched their perfect asses churn as a consequence of very high heels, and possibly because they suspected that they were being watched, and I thought, Lord, Lord, there are these monuments of glory, are there not?

A couple of hours later, there was a gentle rap at my door, and it was the daughter herself, in luscious loose orange-colored silk, leaning against the doorframe.

"My mother said you might need something and asked me to tell you that if there is anything we can bring you, please let us know."

I suspected blackmail immediately. It was simply too good not to be blackmail.

"Well, will you please thank your mother," I said, "and if there turns out to be something, I will certainly remember her kind offer."

The next morning I had to fly to San Francisco, and when I got back four days later they had checked out.

What a fool, I thought. Suppose it *had* been blackmail? What's wrong with that?

On the Hop
with Leonard Lyons

LEONARD LYONS HAD TO SEEK OUT celebrities, it was his work as a daily newspaper columnist. I don't think he ever had a minute for anybody who wasn't a name, but even so, he was a very decent fellow doing his job. I liked to see him table-hopping at Sardi's, and I liked being at his home, where I met Eddie Duchin, the incomparable pianist, and the great Marc Chagall, and even Billy Rose's first boss, Bernard Baruch, who told Billy Rose, "Only horses' asses pay taxes." Bernard Baruch was forever shifting up the gears of his hearing aid to such worshippers as Kitty Carlisle, and down to such skeptics as Jimmy Cannon, who had heard all about Mr. Baruch's advice to Presidents and took the view that the nation must be rather flimsy in structure if at a time of war it had to call in a man who was known as a profiteer and whose best advice was ridiculous. And here Jimmy Cannon would bring out a newspaper clipping and read: "At a time of full engagement of labor in war production it is advisable to bear in mind that certain of the expectations of the people ought not to be entirely ignored—cosmetics do things for the distaff side of the nation which nothing else can do."

"He's getting a cut from the cosmetics industry," Jimmy Cannon insisted, and of course sales jumped, and manufacturers of goo and guck were not instructed to cease and desist in favor of the manufacture of nitroglycerine for bombs.

[147]

The multimillionaire thought quite nicely of himself, and had no time at all for anybody at a party who dared not be an admirer of his age and wealth.

On the other hand, Leonard Lyons was liked by both those who admired Bernard Baruch and those who considered him a fraud. Leonard Lyons was by far the best anecdotist of his day. He started out pretty much at the same time that I did, in 1934, and we rather grew into the scene together.

One night in 1941, before America had got into the War, Leonard Lyons introduced me to Winston Churchill's son, Randolph, at El Morocco, and from there the three of us went to Billy Reed's where Randolph and I continued to put away the booze. Leonard Lyons never touched the stuff, to the end that both his work might be effectively achieved every day and his job might not suddenly seem unbearable.

One of Leonard Lyons' anecdotes: Winston Churchill said to King Faisal of Saudi Arabia, "Your Excellency, I would like you to meet my son Randolph." The Arab king said, "I am honored, and I regret that I cannot introduce you to my four hundred and forty-eight sons."

Over the years I loved the story, and thought, Somehow, somehow, I have got to be able to have the same kind of family. The hell with Christianity, America, monogamy, and all the rest of that baloney, I want a lot of women pregnant by me, so that my sons and my daughters will be the whole human race.

After the War I mentioned this to Leonard Lyons. He smiled and said, "Henry R. Luce was born in China."

"Was his father King Faisal, too?"

"No, a missionary—Episcopalian, I think," Leonard said.

"Of course," I said, "that explains it."

Gerald Kersh, Morris Gest, and Ken McCormick, Alive, Alive, O

LEONARD LYONS ONE NIGHT TOLD me the new writer Gerald Kersh was waiting for him at Billy Reed's, why not go along and meet him?

Kersh was a rather august fellow from England with a very black beard and eyes that seemed to dart about, as if in expectation of sudden disaster, and yet he spoke and laughed in a loud and hearty voice. He suddenly took a dime and put it into his teeth, pressed up with his thumb, removed the dime from his teeth, and invited me to notice that it was neatly bent.

Two days later he telephoned and said, "Can you meet me at Chambord in ten minutes, the publisher Ken McCormick is buying me lunch and he'll buy you lunch too, because he and I have talked about you."

The lunch was great, but unnecessary. If you eat breakfast, lunch is absurd, and in those days I ate breakfast, at the Hampshire House—Cranshaw melon, minute steak rare with O'Brien potatoes, seven or eight cups of coffee with real cream, rye toast, marmalade, and for dessert apple pie à la mode, total cost about two dollars.

As good luck would have it, I had gotten up very early that morning and had gone out for a walk and had stopped at the 57th Street Automat for only three cups of spout coffee at a nickel a cup and three doughnuts, also a nickel apiece, so that by one o'clock when I reached Chambord I was hungry. Taking my cue from Gerald Kersh, I ordered the most expensive stuff—bluepoint oysters, broiled pompano, asparagus, lamb chops with leaf spinach, green salad with Roquefort dressing, mixed cheese, crêpes suzettes, three kinds of wine, and a magnificent strong black coffee, to support the expensive Havana cigars, of which Gerald Kersh took four for his pocket and one for his teeth, and put four in my outside jacket pocket, as I fixed one in my teeth.

The publisher, sensing a charade of some kind, tried not to be surprised, and failed, even if his whole being seemed of an order that was above the showing of any order of surprise. I had expected to see somebody like Morris Gest, with whom I had had a chat in 1928 at the opening in San Francisco of *The Miracle*. I sneaked into the show at the Civic Auditorium, and caught the producer Morris Gest with his Viennese velour hat on his head coming up the center aisle after the show, saying quickly to me, "Come with me over here before high society swallows me up— what about this *Miracle*, what do you think of it?"

He'd never seen me before in his life.

"It's very funny, it's ridiculous, it's a practical joke," I said, "but you've made it seem like the birth of true Christianity, so it's all right."

His dark Romanian face broke out into a big smile, and he said, "Here they come, thank you, but we must speak again."

But of course we never did.

The publisher who bought lunch did not look at all like Morris Gest, he looked like Henry Wallace, Vice-President to Franklin Delano Roosevelt, and then booted out in favor of Harry Truman.

I always admired Ken McCormick of Doubleday, because while Gerald Kersh and I ran up a tab that must have come to a hundred dollars when that was big money, he didn't bat an eye, although he himself declined to follow our example, saying he had had a big breakfast and really wanted only toast and coffee.

Geoffrey Faber, T. S. Eliot,
Herbert Read,
Barnett Freedman
and the Limehouse Blues

CLARIDGES in London has no apostrophe, the same as Finnegans, in Finnegans Wake. The hotel was just down the street from where I was employed in 1944 by the Army at wages of approximately a dollar a day, at 33 Davies Street, Grosvenor Square. I would go to Claridges at least once a day, either to look at the swells in the lounge at tea, to use a writing desk, or to keep an appointment with somebody.

One of the appointments was for lunch with Herbert Read, a tall, muscular, sensitive man who had written a fine book about Eric Gill.

Eric Gill was a remarkable all-around man of life and art, a designer of type, a sculptor, an essayist, and, as I recall, a devout man of prayer.

Inasmuch as Herbert Read and I shared the same London publishing house, Faber & Faber, I had mentioned to Geoffrey Faber my admiration for Herbert Read at lunch at the Ritz a week earlier. Geoffrey Faber was the founder of the firm, and he was *both* of the Fabers in the name.

Or, as T. S. Eliot had put it later on at a lunch at the Connaught, it was thought nicer on the ear to have the name twice.

I had mentioned to the founder that I cherished Faber

books above all others made in London, and considered two things clear, that Barnett Freedman made the finest drawings for book dustjackets, and frontispieces, and that reading Herbert Read on just about any subject was a great pleasure. Not that I cared as he did for the things he wrote about, but there was a kind of comfortable passion in every word he put on paper. That appealed to me, I observed, because I am not really especially concerned about words as words. I care about them *enough* of course, but what I am really after is what I can get them to mean, apart from themselves, or even in spite of themselves.

My admiration was relayed to Herbert Read by Geoffrey Faber and soon thereafter I received a very neat handwritten invitation to lunch on a certain date at about one o'clock but if I couldn't make it, please telephone the previous day, and so on.

I was there at precisely one o'clock and Herbert Read was waiting. Meeting him for the first time, I said, rather as a small joke and almost not expecting even to be heard, "How did you know it was me? From the uniform?"

But his hearing was good and he replied, "No, I think more from the writing."

Continuing my American effort at breaking the ice, with a touch of social eccentricity, I said, "Can you perhaps give me an idea how the buzz bombs never fall on Claridges, the Savoy, or the Dorchester, but always on the crowded houses of Limehouse and the other London slums?"

We sat down at a table set aside for him.

"I have noticed that, also," he said earnestly. "I check the listings of the strikes every day at Charing Cross, as I suspect you do, too, and I have yet to read of a bomb striking a place like this. It is almost embarrassing to be here."

"Perhaps it's a conspiracy," I said.

We took menus and held them while the elegant elderly waiter waited. "Not so much a conspiracy between the parties at war," I went on. "The Germans and the English, for instance, but between unknown witnesses, or the heavenly host."

Herbert Read said, "We are indeed always involved in more than we can ever guess, never mind how much *more* we are involved in at a time of war—it sickens the heart to see how the denied and deprived are now even more denied and deprived, to the point of death."

And so we went on in this manner, holding up the waiter a bit, but not too long for a good London waiter.

It was an excellent meal of wine and fish, salad and coffee and sweet, rather grand for wartime London.

Being one of the richest privates in the American Army I tried of course to pay the check, but Herbert Read insisted on signing it.

He told me about Eric Gill, and then we talked about the poet William Blake, the probable model for Eric Gill, and then I went back to 33 Davies, to my desk and doodling for the duration. And Herbert Read went back to his desk and his doodling, I suppose.

The Limehouse dead of the previous night had been forty-four—they went back to Jesus, most likely. The dead at Claridges only turned over and went back to sleep.

The Biggest Golden Yellow
Rolls-Royce in the World

I SAT BESIDE Anthony Eden at dinner in London, in 1944, when he was very close to Winston Churchill, who was England itself, as Charles de Gaulle was France.

But it *was* Anthony Eden, not Winston Churchill, who appeared to be the classic Englishman. He had the neat clipped moustache, the trim figure, and the cautious and apparently reasonable way of speaking. In short, he was altogether the proper Englishman, a trustworthy and predictable fellow, who therefore seemed to have had nothing but greater fame ahead for himself.

The movies of Hollywood displayed many English actors performing variations of the classic Englishman. C. Aubrey Smith, for instance, was put into very nearly every movie that needed a man who would be instantly accepted as traditional, mainly English, but now and then also royal or upper-class Russian, French, Roman, Greek, Christian, Moslem, or whatever the scenario called for.

There were also Clive Brook, Ronald Colman, Herbert Marshall, and many others who built careers on the inferiority felt so deeply by so many of the people of power in the movie industry, an inferiority somewhat relieved by the hiring (and firing) of the Englishmen, and, later on, Englishwomen.

Having the English at lunch demonstrated the power of the producers both to themselves and to their enemies, generally educated people with big mouths.

[155]

Anthony Eden sat at my right at the head of the table, and around the table we were all kinds, as the saying is.

Quietly, sipping soup, then chomping roast beef with Yorkshire pudding, and tossing salad, and flipping flan for dessert, the man to my left but one came around in the table talk to Armenia, Armenians, myself, my California family, originally from Bitlis, and finally to Michael Arlen, who had long since been out of the glare of fame. Nobody ever mentioned his novel *The Green Hat* any more, made into a play with Katharine Cornell playing the part of Iris March, and into a movie with Greta Garbo.

"Dikran became my friend when he first came down to London from Manchester," the man said. "I was always happy to see him, for he was easy and pleasant company. And then suddenly he became so rich under the name of Michael Arlen that he went and ordered the longest Rolls-Royce ever manufactured. It was golden yellow, and it suited him so well that none of us felt it was outrageous. Only Michael Arlen could make the biggest yellow Rolls-Royce in the world seem precisely right to drive around in London."

I liked that. And I liked believing that the man was not putting himself out about an old acquaintance. I believed that he was not making small talk to one Armenian about another, he was remembering fondly a part of his own youth in London when such things as getting rich on one book and ordering the biggest Rolls-Royce were perfectly natural, sensible, and proper.

Anthony Eden chatted with the lady to his right, and then he chatted with the gentleman to her right, but out of everything that he said the only thing I noticed and now remember was that every now and then he said, "Quite."

"That's class," I thought. "He surely means something else."

From Fortnum & Mason
in Piccadilly to Shaw & Shaw
at Ayot Saint Lawrence

THERE IS an Armenian tailor whose home and place of work is less than two hundred yards as the crow flies from my fifth-floor flat in Paris, where I am writing this book.

He is soon going to Soviet Armenia, not to visit but to live, and when he gets there he wants to write a book called *My Neighbor Saroyan*, so he keeps inviting me to his place for a cup of tea. And while I am at his house he asks questions, and writes on a lined tablet in Armenian, because he wants to get my answers just right, he says.

"Well," I tell him, "it really isn't necessary to get any of this just right, these really aren't the things about myself, or about yourself, or about anybody at all, that make a difference."

"What is, then?" he says, and I say, "Well, the *living* thing of course, that's what takes noticing and is likely to be worth writing about."

"The living thing?" the tailor says. "What's that? What do you mean? I want to get everything you say just right, what *is* the living thing?"

And then suddenly he goes right on and says, "How did you meet Shaw?"

"If you mean George Bernard Shaw," I say, "I met him through an Australian newspaperwoman in London in 1944. She insisted that I must meet the old man. I told her

I didn't want to bother him. I told her I was also supposed to meet Sean O'Casey, another Irishman, who lived down in Devon, but I didn't want to bother him, either. But this lady from Australia went to work and all of a sudden I got a long handwritten letter from Mr. Shaw asking me to take a train three days later at eleven in the morning and to arrive at Ayot Saint Lawrence where his chauffeur would pick me up and drive me to his house, and so that happened. That's how I met him."

"Well," the tailor says, "please tell me about *that*, because Shaw is a great writer, is he not?"

"Yes, of course he is," I say, "but I didn't care about that so much as about the fact that he was alive at all, well along into his eighties, and still saying outrageous things to the English. At the height of the bombing of London, for instance, he piped up to a number of visiting newspaper reporters that Hitler was one of the greatest men in the history of the world, and that everything he was trying to do made sense if you studied such a simple thing as cause and effect, and of course everybody in England, not to mention everybody in France, and America, felt that George Bernard Shaw was a senile, sick old fool. But that was none of my business, either. It was the living thing about him that interested me, and that is why I went to the trouble of going to Fortnum & Mason in Piccadilly to buy him some hothouse grapes, a sweet-smelling golden melon, some figs, some peaches, and a few other things like that."

"What did he say?" the tailor said.

"I'll tell you," I said, "but first you must know that he looked something like a contemporary saint, a white-bearded skinny old geezer in knickers. Second, he sounded like a choirboy. He had a chirpy high-pitched voice. Third, he wanted me to understand that he was a performer, and would soon begin his performance. He did this by saying:

'Armenian? But didn't the Turks *kill* all of the Armenians?' This was said in order to give me fair warning about the working of his mind. Perhaps also to diminish any high regard I might have for his character. I think he suspected that I considered him a kind of saint, and he didn't want to be a saint. But he couldn't fool me, and he remained the gentlest, kindest, the most decent fellow in England, and possibly in the world. And so we sat in the parlor of his house, and this woman, not his wife, brought tea and spice cake for me—he didn't have anything—and I smoked one cigarette after another, even as I gulped down many cups of hot tea and finished all of the slices of spice cake. The woman suddenly discovered the basket of fruit I had left in the hall upon arrival and she said, 'Mr. Shaw, I thought you might like to see what this young American soldier has brought you.' "

" 'This is not a young American soldier,' George Bernard Shaw replied. 'This is the last Armenian in the world, and what's more, he writes plays. Why did you bring me all this food? Why do the Americans think I'm hungry? I'll give it to the neighbors.'

"Oh, he was a card," I said to the tailor, "but he couldn't fool me for one second. I had paid more than twenty-five dollars for the stuff in the basket, and he really enjoyed seeing so much beauty, he just wanted to go right on being a performer, because *that* is the living thing. *Performing*. He was a liar on behalf of style and truth, or at any rate on behalf of a new variation of truth."

"I don't understand," the tailor said, "but let me write that down just as you said it, maybe I will understand it later on, or somebody else will."

A *Star and Garter* Clam Bake and Lobster Feast at Gypsy Rose Lee's Townhouse

Gypsy Rose Lee was a tall girl who spoke with a slight lisp, possibly the consequence of an overbite.

Her mother's name had been Hovick, and she had always had theatrical ambitions for her two daughters, the other being June Havoc.

Gypsy Rose Lee was the star of Mike Todd's Broadway burlesque show *Star and Garter*. And Mike Todd was a cigar-chomping hustler whose home had been somewhere in the Midwest. I had taken him to sit with George Jean Nathan at his corner table at 21 because I believed the elegant drama critic would enjoy the company of a warm-hearted fellow like Mike Todd and at the same time derive other benefits from such an acquaintanceship, benefits not unrelated to Nathan's lifetime fascination with and passion for the theatre, which his pal H. L. Mencken loathed.

The first thing Mike Todd did after drinking with George Jean Nathan was send his young son up to Nathan's apartment at the Royalton Hotel with a case of the whiskey that Nathan seemed to prefer, along with an assortment of other liqueurs of a more exotic order, befitting a man of such elegance. He also sent a basket of imported cheeses and pâtés and such—an outlay bought at a cost of a cool one hundred dollars at a time when such a sum was not thrown about wildly.

George Jean Nathan was delighted by the gesture of

respect and admiration displayed by the showman in rushing his son over with such a bountiful gift.

And so, knowing how smitten by culture the leading lady of his refined burlesque show was, Mike Todd one night took George Jean Nathan and William Saroyan backstage during an intermission to sit and chat with Gypsy Rose Lee. I found her not at all unlike any of the other actresses I had ever met—that is to say, determined to be seen in a good light, excited to the point of almost falling down, slightly perspiring, untidy, giddy, and altogether delightful as something possibly a little better than another demonstration of human eccentricity, out of the necessity to retaliate against parents, nationality, class, religion, environment, schooling, category, and all of the other things that nobody wants to be so burdened with as to be virtually buried by.

She was not a beauty. No wonder the scant costume of the stripteaser appealed to her mother so early in her daughter's life and career. The enactment of the long-legged tease must have seemed precisely right to both mother and daughter as the swiftest and safest way to fame and fortune.

One day she telephoned me at the Hampshire House and asked me to please come right over to her townhouse where a lobster feast was about to begin, and of course I wanted to go, but my cousin Ross Bagdasarian was just in from Fresno, on his way to Army motorcycle school in Providence. Also visiting me was the young girl who had appeared in my last play on Broadway, which being anti-war, was an instant flop, or as Joe Frisco said after watching a run-through, "K-k-k-kid, it won't go. The only hit right now is the War."

I told Gypsy Rose Lee that I'd love to come to the clambake, but my cousin was visiting and so was a young actress.

There was a pause, letting me know that she knew I wanted her to ask me to bring them with me, but also letting me know that she preferred writers and intellectuals, not their cousins and their starlet-type girl friends.

At last she fairly screamed back at me, "Bill, my dear, you just bring along *anybody* you want to bring along."

I looked at the young soldier and at the garish girl I was to marry less than a year later and I thought, Ah, the hell with it, I won't go to the clambake, that's all, and we'll sit here and go on talking and drinking and then we'll go to dinner at the Golden Horn.

But in the end I took them by taxi to the clambake, and they did indeed make the going painful for Gypsy Rose Lee, who was enchanted by Mark Van Doren, the poet and professor, and by George Davis, the novelist and editor, and by dozens of others of that sort, so here suddenly was the loud Armenian from Fresno and his young cousin. What could anybody do with their loud voices and *non sequitur* remarks?

The starlet-type young lady was nothing if not decorous and refined, or at any rate almost refined—although thick purple lipstick did seem a little difficult to put a sensible meaning upon.

Homage to Al Nidevar

I HAVE ALWAYS BEEN a laugher, disturbing people who are not laughers, upsetting whole audiences at theatres. Laughing *can* be a crime, or at any rate a misdemeanor. I once laughed at a judge's remark in a courtroom in San Francisco, and was promptly arrested and taken for questioning to the Chief of Detectives. At a performance in New York of James Thurber's *The Male Animal* I was actually *asked* by an usher sent by the management to stop laughing. I was unable to believe the request. I thought it must be a joke. The theatre was determined not to have a powerful laugher in its audience. (And I believe I know what laughter really is, what Freud and others have decided that it *must* be, but I can't be bothered about that, either.)

I laugh, that's all. I love to laugh. Laughter to me is being alive. I have had rotten times and I have laughed through them. Even in the midst of the very worst times I have laughed. When I went mad in London, a frustrated private in the American Army who had worked night and day to write a novel in thirty-nine days, because I had been promised that this would get me back to New York on furlough, and I was cheated out of that furlough, exhausted and desperate, and gone off the rocker, I still laughed. The mad also laugh, or is that what Freud and the others discovered perhaps, that *only* the mad laugh?

Well, even so, I prefer the company of laughers. I find people who respond to my stories and my laughter are the people I trust. That is how I felt about Al Nidevar at Emerson School when we were nine or ten years old.

Al Nidevar seemed to know that his parody recitations of *Hiawatha* would not be wasted if I heard them. He had an astonishing ability to respond to my laughter with new variations of mimicry and mockery, new turns of language, new usages of voice, and new facial expressions. All of which for one whole winter made me roar with laughter in the playground of Emerson School, now and then joined by my old pal Eddie Emerian.

Other boys watched and listened and said, "What are you guys laughing about? What's so funny about *Hiawatha?*"

Well, of course that was just it. Either *Hiawatha itself* is funny, or it isn't. And as far as I was concerned, and as far as Al Nidevar was concerned, it wasn't necessary to do very much more than speak the lines precisely as written by Henry Wadsworth Longfellow for the words to be hilarious.

Al Nidevar's enunciation and voice made language itself inexhaustibly comic.

I wish to God he had gone on with it, but Al Nidevar stayed put, first in the house on South Van Ness, down near the famous Arch with the word *Fresno* in 88 electric light bulbs, down near Railroad Avenue, a house owned by his mother Mary, a widow, and occupied also by his big brother Mark, who was my brother Henry's age. And then Al Nidevar for years kept his job operating the elevator at the Mattei Building, which I saw built, selling papers across the street at Fresno and Fulton Streets, just down a bit from the Kinema Theatre, where I got in free of charge every day to see special parts of special movies like *Shoulder Arms* with Charlie Chaplin, who was knighted in 1975 by the Queen of England, sitting in a wheelchair held by Oona O'Neill.

And nobody made the world laugh louder than Charlie Chaplin, the genius whose materials were loneliness, secret love, hunger, poverty, speed, imagination, poetry, and finesse—a real talent for cleaning the fingernails at table (alone) without offending God, and an ability to kick a cop and run that was never matched by anybody else in reality or imagination.

Al Nidevar stayed put, and then disappeared, but for a while he was as great as Charlie Chaplin himself.

John McCormack Singing
Everlasting Ireland,
Your Eyes Have Told Me So

I NEVER MET JOHN MCCORMACK but I wish I had, because he sang certain songs as nobody else in the world has ever sung them. James Joyce had the highest regard for him, as he had for the songs that John McCormack sang, several of which figure importantly in the story of Dublin, and of the human race.

One song he sang is *Your Eyes Have Told Me So*, and to me it is one of the great songs of all time, notwithstanding that it was written by a couple of professional New York Tin Pan Alley boys of sixty or seventy years ago. I used to know their names, from a phonograph record I happened to own, but I have never been able to tell which of the two wrote the words, and which the music.

I once told Billy Rose that I thought it was clever of him to have written the song *Barney Google*, and he accepted the praise. He didn't say that he hadn't written any part of the song, that he had got his name up there with the writers, and received one third of the song's earnings, because he had put the song into one of his Broadway shows.

There seem to have been quite a few third parties who got their names up there that way. Al Jolson probably came nearest to deserving a third interest in any song he sang because his style of singing was so unique, certainly nobody else could do it *that* way. And so if he sang a song, it became a hit.

But when my cousin Ross Bagdasarian and I made up a song called *Come On-a My House*, which Rosemary Clooney sang to Mitch Miller's arrangement, both of us actually wrote both the words and music. And it couldn't be said that one of us did more on the music, or the words, than the other. We were both illiterates in music, but we *could* sing, or at any rate holler, and of course that song is a kind of hollering American song based upon hollering Armenian music.

In addition to *Your Eyes Have Told Me So*, there are other songs that nobody in the world can sing the way John McCormack sings them, for every time you listen to one of his recordings, you hear a great man singing with all the living breath of the human race.

The sentiment of *Your Eyes Have Told Me So* is just right for John McCormack's genius and style. Well, you can't call it style so much as what it really is, his lucky helplessness. He sang bel canto, they say, and that means he studied with the Italians, most likely. I remember once being asked by somebody if it could be said that Ross Bagdasarian sang bel canto and I had to reply, "Well, maybe, but it is really more nearly Eddie Canto." But I wasn't shot on the spot, probably because I wasn't understood.

If you study the career of John McCormack, you learn that on discs he has all sorts of great stuff that he sang in operas, and he does that stuff absolutely beautifully, but to me, at least, the operatic stuff can't compare with what he does with plain simple Irish tunes, and with various Tin Pan Alley achievements.

He was a people's singer, and he gave their songs both body and soul.

I came *near* meeting John McCormack, though, and I cherish that truth, that meaninglessness, or that near moment of great meaning, whichever it may be, which accounts for my bringing up the matter at all.

It was in the fall of 1933 and I was out in the streets of San Francisco with a couple of dollars in my pocket. I ran into Kid Jazz from Fresno. We began casing coffee shops and saloons of the tenderloin for pickups, at which he was very good. Waitresses were terribly flattered by his patient small talk steadily moving into the boudoir.

At one saloon on Turk Street the bartender said that John McCormack had just left the place, after singing a chorus of something about a broken-down old house of somebody's lost childhood.

We gulped down our beer and went out into the street to look for the singer, because the bartender had the feeling that John McCormack was going to visit a few other bars in the neighborhood before calling it a night.

We went to about a dozen bars, and at one of them we were told that John McCormack had indeed been there and had done a chorus of *I Hear You Calling Me*, but had gone on. We didn't stop looking until around two in the morning when we paid a visit to something weird called a dance marathon.

I never saw John McCormack, but I heard him, and I still do.

He sings everlasting Ireland, as Armenak Shah-Mouradian sings everlasting Armenia.

The Alphabet Opera
by Paul Bowles
and William Saroyan

PAUL BOWLES, who is famous less as a composer than as a novelist, did the music for my first play, *My Heart's in the Highlands*. I was delighted by his haunting arrangement of W. B. Courtney's music for the song of the same name, which I had first sung at Longfellow Junior High School in Fresno. Now and then Paul Bowles and I talked about collaborating on a whole work of some kind for the theatre, perhaps not a musical comedy in the Broadway sense, but some kind of American play with music, or even some mixture of play, opera, and ballet.

One evening in the days when I was staying at the Great Northern Hotel, a waltz melody came into my head and wouldn't leave. The next morning it was still there, so I telephoned Paul Bowles and said, "Paul, I've got this crazy waltz going in my head. If I take a taxi down to your place in the Village, will you put it on paper for me, so it won't be lost? I can fit appropriate words to it later on, and of course it will be music by Paul Bowles and words by William Saroyan."

"Well," he said, "I don't know, but come along, let's find out what it is that you have."

So I went out and grabbed a taxi and in ten or eleven minutes I was in the street outside Paul's place. I turned away from the world to gather my musical self together, to summon up all of the reality of the waltz, and to render it as effectively as possible in the limited terms of *da da, da da, dee dee, da da, da da, dee, da, da, da.* I went through the whole thing, far better than I had imagined I might be able to do, believing in it, and becoming the equivalent of a performer of a classic work of music.

Upstairs, I did the whole thing again, for Paul Bowles. It took a good full thirty seconds or so, I suppose, for there is virtually no theme in music, however magnificent, that in the first place endures longer than eight seconds or so, let alone thirty. It is the second usage of the theme that makes the symphony, concerto, aria, or whatever it might be, so meaningful, and exciting, and satisfying. And then the third usage, and the fourth, followed by numberless variations and new elements that are added to the theme, all of which I was sure had been provoked in the brilliant creative mind of Paul Bowles by my *da da, da da, dee, da da* rendition of the great song that had come to me like a golden gift straight from Roseland Ballroom, 1922.

"It's no good," Paul Bowles said very quietly. "I don't write music like that. I can't."

But to this day I wish Paul Bowles had been bowled over by that waltz and had written it, so that people all over the world, but especially at the Annual Ball in Vienna, could get out there and waltz around to it forever.

And then, seven or eight years later, he wrote to me from Mexico City and suggested that perhaps now we might do an opera together. But in San Francisco at that time I was in the biggest fight to the death that I have ever been in— with everybody and everything. But of course I didn't want to write back and tell him I couldn't do anything in the way of a story or a line for an opera right now because I was fighting the world, the mad wife, her mother, the two kids, the Tax Collector, Jesus, Abraham Lincoln, and anybody else I happened to think of or meet, and so I told Paul Bowles in a rather enthusiastic letter that I had just the book for a real opera at last: *The Alphabet Opera.*

A, being a vowel, would be a soprano. She would come out looking all A, and would give out with a grand high statement of the first letter, and stop. And then say it for a wholebeat, like AAAAAA, and then high, then medium, then low, and so on.

Next B, a tenor. He would come out looking exactly like B, and he would fool around with B for a while.

And thus, before long we would have ourselves the first original opera in the history of music. Wouldn't we?

Paul Bowles didn't answer for such a long time that I imagined his astonishment by remembering how the famous waltz had affected him.

Finally, though, he wrote a brief note and said, "Well, I've been thinking about it, but there just doesn't seem to be enough in the idea for an opera."

Too bad.

He wrote a one-line letter, and I lost a whole opera.

Writers and Writers
and Writers

ELIO VITTORINI BEGAN to write to me in San Francisco from Rome soon after my second book, *Inhale and Exhale*, was published, in 1936. And he let me know that he was translating my stuff into Italian as it appeared.

He is of course the distinguished writer, famous in all of Italy, especially for a book entitled *In Sicily*.

Elio Vittorini also wrote to Ernest Hemingway, and also translated Mr. Hemingway's short stories and perhaps his novels, and Mr. Hemingway in turn wrote a foreword to one of Mr. Vittorini's books.

Almost every new writer, not only in the United States, but in the whole world, apparently wrote to Ernest Hemingway and asked him to write a foreword to his book, and I have always considered Mr. Hemingway's courtesy toward these people exemplary.

I have read two or three of his forewords, and I have enjoyed reading them, although they could have been a little less momentous, for many of the writers turned out to be more skilled at writing to other writers asking them to write forewords than at writing stuff likely to make them famous enough to have newer writers someday write to them asking for forewords.

I, also, have been asked to write forewords, and I have written several of them. One involved a pit boss at the

Rancho Vegas in 1949. He would come over to the bar whenever he saw me there, and chat about writing, not gambling. It turned out of course that he worked in Las Vegas only for the money and that his real work was writing, and that as soon as his work earned him some reasonably big money he was going to leave Las Vegas and write full time.

He said he had a neatly typed novel that he would like me to read, and a few days later he came to the bar and placed beside my glass about three hundred pages of thick white paper covered with triple-spaced typing with wide margins, so that if it was a question of reading what he had written, it was certainly visually convenient, but I said, "Well, I'm drinking right now, so let me take this home after I'm finished, and we'll see."

He said, "You know, Bill, a good strong foreword by you would not only get me a publisher, it would make the book a success."

I said, "I doubt it, but let's just wait and see."

Around half-past four that morning I took the bundle to my cottage back of the casino and set it on the bureau. I glanced only at the title, which was something like *Ginger Slater*. I then read the name of the writer himself, also phony, along the lines of Clayton Sherbourne, so I wasn't much encouraged. Then I read the dedication: "To Marge, you know why, dear."

I groaned and thought, No, I'd better not try to read this now, I'll try tomorrow afternoon before I go to the casino for coffee and the day's first drink.

In the end, I wrote the foreword to *Ginger Slater* by Clayton Sherbourne without reading beyond the first seven or eight words, which I now refuse to even try to approximate. The first thing I said in the foreword was that I hadn't read the novel and was never going to read it, but

[173]

I was writing the foreword because I had promised the writer that I would.

Ginger Slater was published, but Clayton Sherbourne didn't leave Las Vegas, and I have no idea what happened to Marge.

Greta Garbo at the
Little Woman's Big Party
on North Rodeo Drive

SHE CAME INTO the house on North Rodeo Drive in Beverly Hills, full of people drinking and eating, and with her was her friend John Gunther, and his wife Jean, who had indeed won her over to the idea of going out to a private *party*, and she was precisely the lady the rest of the world had seen only in films: Greta Garbo.

She seemed even more exciting in person than in film. She went straight to Charlie Chaplin, who was sitting demurely beside his recent bride, Oona, and she said, "Oh, Charlie Chaplin, Charlie Chaplin," and nobody ever heard anything more astonishing or right, or more simply spoken.

But what did it mean? Well, of course it meant that in the fable of the human race in the human world, there were these unaccountable luminaries who in saying nothing to one another nevertheless say everything, and understand perfectly.

She was then perhaps forty-eight years of age, and had long since done her last movie, which hadn't meant very much to her, or to the producers of the movie, or to the bankers, or to the exhibitors of movies, and worst of all to the buyers of tickets.

Greta Garbo, in her last three or four movies, had still been Greta Garbo, but this truth had begun to signify less and less to the human race of the Western World at large, and almost nothing to the Eastern World.

It was my house, but I never gave a party in my life. The party was the production of the wife, just lately married to me a second time, in 1950, no longer trying to make a life on Taraval Street in San Francisco, or on West 59th Street in New York, just up from the Plaza, but apparently trying to make a splash in Hollywood with a big party costing me a couple of thousand dollars.

She knew she could count on her old pal Oona from girlhood days in New York to bring her husband Charlie Chaplin, and if John Gunther could bring Greta Garbo, then that would really make it a triumph, wouldn't it?

Well, there were at least a hundred people in the house, and overflowing onto the front lawn, and out into the back garden, and the tennis court—after the lease ran out the owner of the house, Jan Kiepura's father-in-law, sued me and was given a judgment of a couple of thousand dollars over and above the high rent, because somebody had spilled champagne on his wallpaper here and there, and some kids had made crayon marks in other places.

It was a noisy party, and nobody was noisier than the host—myself. I was drunk before the first guest arrived, but I can drink and go right on being polite better than anybody I know, or anybody I have seen in action.

I had heard that Greta Garbo might come, just might at the last minute decide to come, although she had told John Gunther, "Oh, no, no, I do not go to parties, I can't stand parties, it is bad enough trying to speak to people one at a time, to dear friends, even."

And so there she was suddenly speaking to Charlie Chaplin.

Were they old friends? Lovers? Had they worked together in a movie? Well, little by little it became clear that no, really, all it was was her own recognition of the fabulous reality of Charlie Chaplin in the human story of the brave little man in the hard big world. And she simply had to let him know.

Later, in New York, and in Paris, I saw her at similar private parties, and she was always the person who looked at everything and everybody, as she always had at lovers in movies, with a pity that was ravishing, and said, "Oh, you poor poor poor soul, will you never stop being pathetic and stupid?" That was the secret of her love scenes, and her success.

Let's Just Nobody Ever Forget Joan Castle

JIMMY CANNON was a sportswriter who had real style.

The fact is he never wrote a column that was not full of amazing turns of English, very near poetry and seldom without wit.

The year after my first two plays appeared on Broadway and I had noticed how much more money a writer could earn from plays, and how much more attention the press paid to plays than to novels, I asked him, "Have you ever thought of writing a play? It's not nearly as hard as any writer is apt to feel who hasn't tried. Maybe you ought to give it a go."

The sportswriter said, "Well, I don't know, like I know sports, so who am I to write plays?"

He was the first person I ever heard say such a thing, long before the use of the word *like* became popular, especially among the inarticulate.

He affected being a kind of Damon Runyon Broadway character, while his writing demonstrated that he was a very different kind of person entirely.

For years he had a large room at the Edison Hotel on 47th Street just west of Broadway, and this was all he wanted in the way of house and home.

He loved to telephone. I have always hated using the telephone, hated the loud ringing bell, hated the fire-alarm intrusion of it at any hour, as if a terrible disaster were being cleverly averted in the nick of time by the electric apparatus of the international telephone system.

I have never received a telephone call that justified the excitement and fuss of the electronics involved. If I can't see somebody I love, for instance, such as a daughter, or a son, I would rather receive a letter.

Consequently, whenever Jimmy Cannon telephoned I tried to find an excuse to cut him short.

Once, when I was at the Hampshire House and quite comfortable and not in the midst of writing, however, I let him go on, and soon discovered that he was eating as he spoke, and taking sips of coffee. The call continued for just under an hour.

He knew many people, and he gathered together all kinds of remarks he had heard them make, which he passed along to other acquaintances, and then laughed as if to applaud himself. It was hearty laughter that nevertheless always sounded slightly spurious, but of course really wasn't at all.

One of the remarks he made on the telephone once had to do with the photograph of a gangster on the front page of the New York *Post*.

The mobster's eyes were almost shut: "Point a camera at a killer and he's more terrified than if it was a gun."

"Gangsters and playboys," he said. "They're both camera shy, and you can never see their eyes in their photographs."

And he roared with laughter, as if to ask, "Was that perceptive and brilliant, what I just said? Or wasn't it?"

And then one day while he and I and Jed Harris were walking from Billy LaHiff's to Lindy's, Jimmy Cannon said, "Last night Clifford Odets came up to me at Toots Shor's and he said, 'Jimmy, I wrote about you in my journal this morning.' I didn't know what to say. Should I have said, 'Gee, thanks loads, I guess I'm famous now. I'm in your journal. When is it coming out? My own stuff always comes out tomorrow, will your journal come out after you've been dead fifty years, or what?' "

We pretended to be arguing about a pretty girl named Joan Castle at Sardi's one night, when she suddenly said, "Look, I need the publicity, do me a good turn, go out to the street and have a fight about me—Leonard Lyons is here, and he'll report it. And Arto Demirjian is here with his camera, and he'll photograph it. And it'll be on the front pages all over the country. And I'll be famous. Will you? Please?"

Like a couple of laughing fools we left the corner table at Sardi's and went out to 44th Street and squared off, and suddenly Jimmy Cannon said, "I'm not going to do it."

"Why not?" I said.

"Well," he said, "like if it was for religious art or abandoned babies, it might be all right, but Joan Castle's not in a play, and she hasn't just published a book, so what's the publicity going to be *for*?"

James Victor Joseph Cannon was a street writer with more than a touch of greatness, who at least figuratively died in his introspective room at the Edison Hotel, off the phone, and in total truth and silence.

A book of his writings will some day be published, and be a revelation.

A Gentleman and a Poker Player, George Stevens

GEORGE STEVENS has died—from politeness, I should imagine: thoughtfulness about others, generosity, and all of the other decencies that any man may be permitted to believe he can acquire, and a few men have no way of thrusting out of themselves. George was such a man, but the report in the Paris *Herald* only said he was a movie director.

Well, he certainly directed several movies that are forever great.

His version of Theodore Dreiser's novel *An American Tragedy*, called *A Place in the Sun*, is one of the best movies ever made.

In London, in poker games with foreign correspondents, *Time, Life,* and *New Yorker* correspondents, high-ranking and low-ranking officers, from Generals to Second Lieutenants, and from Corporals to Privates, Colonel George Stevens played the most effective poker I have ever seen. In the course of eleven or twelve games, it is impossible not to notice such a thing.

Being the commanding officer of a photographic unit involving two or three dozen men, including myself, whenever George Stevens noticed that members of his outfit were losers in a game, he would pick up their I.O.U.'s and pay them off out of his winnings. And then while their backs were turned, he would tear up their I.O.U.'s and throw them away.

And of course during a game, hour after happy hour, they were the loud braggarts, and I was the loudest, while George Stevens quietly sat and sipped whiskey, and then suddenly from nowhere took the biggest pot of the night with something unbelievably magnificent or astonishingly paltry, but not so paltry that it didn't beat the other gambler's hand.

One afternoon another member of the photographic unit asked me the amount of my I.O.U. that George Stevens had picked up early that morning, after our first London poker game.

"Eight hundred dollars," I said. "How much was yours?"

"Not quite that bad," the other man said, "but not very good, either. Six hundred. Does George expect us to pay?"

"I don't know," I said, "but I'm handing him my check for eight hundred dollars this afternoon."

About an hour later we both handed George Stevens our personal checks for the I.O.U.'s he had picked up and paid off.

"Well, I want to thank you boys," he said. And he carefully folded the checks and put them in his wallet.

But he never put the checks through and a month later I brought the matter up.

"Colonel Stevens, permission to talk, please."

"Private Saroyan, permission denied."

"Well, anyhow," I said, "I always pay my gambling debts. I'd sooner not pay the grocer. That check for eight hundred dollars hasn't gone through."

"Willie," George Stevens said, "you don't play poker, you play art, you play religion, you play comedy, and any man who takes your money is a son of a bitch, that's all. You know *how* to play to win, but you refuse to bother."

"All right," I said. "Just tell me this. What made *you* learn to bother?"

"Being laughed at by some old-time gamblers in Sacramento," George said. "I was wearing tennis shoes, you see, eighteen years old, green, funny-looking, and they not only laughed at me, they took half my stake of fifty dollars in five minutes. I made up my mind right then and there to make those wise old gentlemen correct their contemptuous opinion of me. It took me from four in the afternoon until midnight to destroy the lot of them. I got up and cashed in all of my chips, almost six hundred dollars, still wearing my tennis shoes, still eighteen years old, still green, still funny-looking, and I moved as politely as possible as I left the place and went home and ate a beautiful meal that my mother had left on the kitchen table. And then I went to bed and slept the sweet sleep of the winner."

He was the wearer of a head that seemed squashed at the back to make a bulge at the front, and a face somewhat crowded with unrelated features, all made handsome by the deep courtesy and intelligence of his eyes—until he played poker, when he kept all that courtesy either deeply concealed or dangerously deceptive.

Orphan in Tears

═══════════════════════════════════

SHE WAS in the bathroom after a bath, and I was in the parlor of a tiny bungalow in back of somebody's Hollywood house, the sort of thing put up to accommodate a sudden guest. I could hear her breathing, or so I thought, and I wondered why she wasn't humming or singing or laughing, and how long would she be.

After ten minutes I began to get ideas—the girl is getting herself delicious for me, that's all.

But after twenty minutes I decided, The girl is either mean or sick to expect anybody to sit in a dismal parlor waiting for her, what's the matter with her?

After thirty minutes of hearing her breathing, or thinking I heard it, fighting off irritation, annoyance, anger, outrage, a feeling of being deliberately belittled by a silly ambitious girl, I thought, Well, now, it's too late, I've got to find out what goes on here, who this is, and what this is about.

A friend of mine had interviewed her for a movie magazine, and she had told him to please arrange for me to meet her.

And then about a month later I was at a summer evening outdoor picnic at the home of a friend, and there she was, accompanied by a famous director who invited me to ride back to town in his car, and between us sat this girl.

By that time I had discovered that she was very eager to

get into the finer world, as somebody must have put it to her, the world of literature, for instance, and as a matter of fact she spoke about Dostoyevsky, and from the odd silence of the director I gathered that he had put her in touch with that mighty writer.

The director was returning to New York in a day or two, and in bringing us together I got the impression that he would like me and this ambitious young lady to go on meeting, now that we had spent forty minutes chatting in a car, but of course that was speculation and in any case irrelevant, and I didn't think I would be very likely to see her again.

To begin with, my second marriage to the same woman, on behalf of a small son and a smaller daughter, and indeed on behalf of the woman herself, and also on behalf of myself, and on behalf of the revived fantasy of founding a family, had again become impossible. I knew she was seeing the world-famous divorce lawyer Jerry Geisler, and that only rotten times were ahead. I lived at a hotel, and I missed the boy and the girl, and I worried about them, and I owed the Tax Collector so much money I didn't see how I'd ever be able to pay him off, and my writing wasn't bringing me any money, and I was drinking a lot because I wanted to, and every morning when I got up to start a day I was more like a dead man than a live man. I wasn't really in any proper shape to take on a strange girl who wanted a number of things known or knowable and a number that were surely as unknown, as unknowable, as things wanted might ever be.

So there I was in the little parlor waiting for her to emerge from the bathroom, going a little berserk because she *wasn't* emerging and wasn't speaking and *was* apparently just barely breathing.

When she came out she was fully clothed and spoke in a

sorrowful whisper, asking me to please not mind the time she had needed to take—and I knew instantly that it wasn't meanness at all, it was something more complicated, and something not for me to try to help her with.

The director was supposed to be good at that sort of thing, at least when it came up in plays, so if he hadn't been able to help her, it wasn't likely that I would.

And of course any illusion of having been compelled to wait in order to behold a ravishing sex-bomb was totally dispelled.

I took her to a circus, but after only half an hour of finding the stuff unbearable I asked if she would mind if we left. We went to the Hot Dog Show for hot-dogs and soda-pop, and we talked, and a month later I took her home and got in bed with her to find her sobbing like a small abandoned child, and a week later she said she was going to meet Joe DiMaggio, and I said, "He just might do it."

An *Omnibus*
of Crazy Playwrights,
Social Historians,
and Funny Comedians

I DIRECTED two great comedians in a television play entitled *Vive* for a Sunday-afternoon live showing on a program called *Omnibus*, in which Alistair Cooke in his soft-spoken English (which John O'Hara for some reason found lispy) acted as all-around guide. It was a variety show of ninety minutes' duration including commercials. The Ford Foundation was underwriting the show, which was considered right smart of them, as the saying is. The year was probably 1954.

I have always admired good comedians, but I have known a lot of comedians who haven't been good. Almost any comedian, however, is worth two of just about any other kind of show-biz character, since the purpose of the comedian is to make people laugh. It doesn't matter that very nearly every effective comedian is an unhappy man, or at any rate at least as unhappy as other men. Of course comedians really want to be loved. As if Jesus, who probably wasn't really a comedian, didn't. Or as if anybody doesn't.

Wanting to be loved has somehow in America come to be the terrible mark of the comedian, and the theory is that the greater the comedian the greater the desire, and presumably the greater the failure to have the desire fulfilled.

Comedians shamelessly ask, or if they are clever at their work, *demand* that they be loved, at least while they are performing.

A man like Zero Mostel (I was about to write Zero Monstel) is so strange-looking at first glance, and not especially unstrange-looking at second and third glance, a strangely shaped head, a badly arranged assortment of irregular features which simultaneously seem to be short of something and oversupplied with something else, shadows or hints of other noses, eyes, ears, lips, foreheads, or hair, torso, arms, legs, all distorted, a man who has become a genius of improvisation, of timing, of acceleration, of slowing down, a man like Zero Mostel seems too powerful, too intellectual, too ugly to be willing to beg for love, but in the end one is obliged to reflect that his whole performance is a demand for love so strident and unrelenting that it becomes either unbearable or irresistible.

He himself has remarked that his father wanted him to be a rabbi, and one notices that he might very well have been one, since in his comedy there is the fervor of profound faith.

The producer of *Omnibus* was a man named Robert Saudek who had been a roommate of James Agee at school in the Ivy League somewhere. James Agee had found out that early in 1952 I had written thirteen or fourteen half-hour plays which I intended to introduce on television in my own program, something along the lines of *The Wonderful World of William Saroyan*, a title which in the early 1950s was something permissible but since then has become absurd.

A big-money legal outfit came into the picture, but when I examined the papers I had signed in full and traditional stupidity, I informed the company that I didn't want to get rich, and the deal was canceled.

James Agee told Robert Saudek I had the plays, and indeed showed him eight or nine of them, which he had borrowed from me and forgotten to hand back.

That is how I had six short plays on the opening season of *Omnibus*, and how a year or two later I came to direct two very great comedians in *Vive*: Bert Lahr was vinegar that seemed to want to be wine, and Bobby Clark was a kind of puppy dog that ran about continuously in a state of inexpressible joy, with flashes of doubt and perplexity. The play seemed just right for them together.

That's all. I guided them into this little play set on the Rue La Fayette in Paris, and each of them gave a magnificent performance, seen by a lot of sleepy Sunday afternoon TV watchers. They made me laugh with simple happiness about the inexhaustible enthusiasm of the human race for more folly, inaccuracy, error, and ignorance.

That's all.

Spyros Skouras, Nikita Khrushchev, Preston Sturges, Gregory Ratoff, Humphrey Bogart, and Darryl Zanuck

I MET DARRYL ZANUCK in Paris in May of 1959 when I went to his apartment at the Plaza-Athenée to keep an appointment, to tell him I was broke, owed the Tax Collector a lot of money, and therefore needed to earn a lot.

He listened to my story, told in well under a minute, half-smiled, glanced at his two stooges, and said, "You've got a deal. Forget your bill at the George Cinq, we'll pick up that tab. And let's meet here again tomorrow—no, tomorrow I'm taking Juliette to Deauville—let's meet here day *after* tomorrow at about four o'clock. At that time we'll talk about writing."

He considered himself a writer, and I was therefore glad that he was now in charge of the spending of money on behalf of Twentieth Century-Fox Films. Darryl Zanuck had replaced Spyros Skouras, who in a hearty exchange with Nikita Khrushchev visiting Hollywood had shouted proudly, "I'm a poor Greek boy and the President of Twentieth Century-Fox Films. Only in America could such a thing happen."

Nikita Khrushchev had shouted back, "Nonsense, I am a poor Ukrainian boy, and the Premier of the U.S.S.R."

Soon after that exchange, but surely not on account of it, Spyros Skouras was out, and Darryl Zanuck was in.

Actually, he was only *elevated* a short distance to the position that Spyros Skouras had enjoyed for so long, but the elevation hadn't been the consequence of any intrigue on the part of Darryl Zanuck, it had happened because other people with other axes to grind had wanted it to happen.

Darryl Zanuck was a short man, with a rather dainty waxed white moustache above the kind of teeth one sees when a rabbit nibbles lettuce leaves. He was about fifty-five years old at the time, and I was just fifty. He smoked long Havana cigars that cost a dollar apiece. Perhaps two dollars. Certainly now, in 1976, they must cost three dollars—if you can get them at all.

Darryl Zanuck knew he *appeared* to be throwing money around, especially on writers, but he also knew that the most damage he could do to the financial structure of the movie company by hiring writers would be insignificant in comparison with the money spent by the other departments of the company.

This impressed me, and compelled my respect.

Preston Sturges, for the last four or five years of his life was financed by Darryl Zanuck. Having lived lavishly since the Broadway run of his one successful play (about a girl from East Orange who turned down the proposition of a rich dirty local man in favor of the love of a poor clean New York writer, a play called *Strictly Dishonorable*), and having gone through a couple of million dollars, most of it lost in his big club on Hollywood Boulevard called The Players, where the old prizefighter Tim Moran with his hoarse voice was the gentle-hearted bouncer, and Harry Rosenthal played the piano, and where I used to take my bride-to-be for drinks and food and even to dance, and where Humphrey Bogart, dancing with his third wife Mayo Methot, came cruising by to lisp, "Saroyan, you are the rottenest dancer I've ever seen, after *me*, that is," and danced away rather smartly, I thought—while his wife giggled. Darryl Zanuck looked after Preston Sturges during that writer's last years in Paris, and once said, "He was very depressed near the end. He didn't understand why nobody wanted his writing any more."

I was also moved by Darryl Zanuck's devotion to another old friend, Gregory Ratoff, when the big, burly, loud, cheerful Russian knew he would soon be dead from cancer and therefore tried especially hard to keep up a good front, but now and then suddenly couldn't, and burst into tears, whereupon Darryl Zanuck would say, "Cut that out. You've seen everything. *Twice.*"

And Gregory Ratoff would instantly laugh and bellow back, "Dat's right, Darryl."

A lot of writers hate Darryl Zanuck, and sometimes, remembering something or other in my dealings with him, I do, too, but he was really a good man, and I refuse not to say so.

The Secret of Marc Chagall

THE SECRET OF MARC CHAGALL is the color blue, and sorrow with joy—bright blue, that is, poster blue, American-flag blue, a banal color until it appears in one of Chagall's canvases with his other colors surrounding it, whereupon it is something else entirely, a kind of soul-smiling.

The sorrow with joy is best understood by looking at one of his brides floating above Vitebsk with lovely exposed white breast, high above a sad street, and its sweet houses, above a goat, a cow, a rooster, a hen, and flowers, near a full moon, above a rabbi, and some boys and girls, a bride with long black hair, alive, alive, Chagall paints remoteness, segregation, the patience and power created by the segregation, by the rejection of the whole tribe by the people of that nation, by the government, by the establishment, by the socially superior but spiritually inferior ones.

There is no comparable joy in any other painter's work of the twentieth century. Look for it and you will not find it. Marc Chagall is a small boy in the mourning, sacred and humorous human race, his father's son, his mother's darling. His paintings literally *say* the word *darling.* Everybody says something tender to everybody else. The violins play love, the cantors sing it, the rooftop goats and dreamers say it to the moon and stars. His flag-blue remembers open sky and sanctuary in the midst of menace itself, his accordion players dance defiance to destruction. Nobody else can do, has ever done, what he does.

Leonard Lyons took me one day in the middle 1960s in Paris to call on a friend of his named Manny Sachs. I saw a fragile little old gentleman in a very neat studio somewhere in the best part of the Latin Quarter, as it used to be called. And I was surprised to see paintings that instantly identified themselves as Jewish, and were *not* unlike the paintings of Marc Chagall—and then, after only a moment, were altogether *unlike* them. There is no need ever to rate artists, but this good fellow, apparently in his late seventies, did not have in his magnificent paintings that secret that is in the paintings of Marc Chagall—and the secret is really not blue at all, or sorrow with joy, or love, or darling, or the deliverance of the mortal soul from the limitations of the body.

The secret is many things, which in the end are beyond accounting. As well account for who begats who in the forgetfulness of passion. You get what you get, the world gets what it gets, himself gets himself, and a lifetime is required to know who it was. You could ask of everybody you know, referring to himself of course, who is it? And neither he nor you would ever come within a million light years of anything like a usable truth.

Manny Sachs in his paintings was sombre, almost silent, instead of boisterous and bright, brighter than the brightness of light itself, if such a thing is possible. And in art let us not forget that anything is possible if there is somebody to see to it—helplessly, of course.

Surely Marc Chagall didn't *learn* how to do it, it was always there, so that when he took up brush to put paint upon canvas, it *had* to turn out to be who he was, it had to be himself.

When Sylvia Lyons telephoned me at the Royalton

Hotel at 44 West 44th Street in New York, before or after I had met Manny Sachs I can't say, and asked me to dinner, I had no idea one of the guests would be Marc Chagall.

When I saw him I began to think and guess a little more about his paintings. Every artist is *in* everything he creates, and indeed if the truth is told, every person is *in* his life, in his work, whatever his work may be, and this is visible in his face, figure, stance, movement, and totality. In the lean, loving, witty face of Marc Chagall at dinner that night I saw all of his paintings, all of his life, all of his truth —and thanked God that he had been able to make such a gentle message acceptable to such a violent world—and not only acceptable but sought out, prized, and collected. He was a boy. He was delighted by life. His beloved first wife had lately died, but here he was with a new one, and she seemed to be his first wife all over again. And I had to think about *that*, too. Had she always been precisely right for Marc Chagall, or did she *become* so?

Manny Sachs died a few years after I met him, as I felt when I met him that he soon must. But even when he dies, Marc Chagall is going to escape death, not because of his paintings alone, but for other good and valid reasons, if you know what I mean. And it isn't that it's a secret, it's just that it *is* an edge beyond English, or for that matter any language.

Benjamin Kubelsky of Waukegan, Rich and Famous at a Hollywood Party

I FIRST MET JACK BENNY at a Hollywood party, which is where almost everybody in Hollywood first meets.

Claudette Colbert was also there, straight out of *It Happened One Night*, but now she was not with Clark Gable, she was with her husband, who was some kind of doctor of noses and had done the nose of a cousin of mine.

George Burns was also there, making Jack Benny laugh by not saying anything, by only looking as if he *might* say something.

And at the party there was this woman, and that man, and that woman, and this man, and everybody was glittering, everybody had prepared for the party. Every wife wanted to be the star of the party, and every husband had been thrilled to spare no expense to help his woman in her ambition.

The paintings on the walls of the house were worth at least three million dollars, and the glassware *was* glassware, so that when a drink was fixed for you, and you accepted it, and you took a sip, you tasted wealth right there at the rim of the sparkling glass with the glass-clean ice in it, and the super-smooth Scotch, and you let it go, you let the absurdity of it all go, the only right thing in human reality was the Hollywood party, and in between was only rehearsal time. Be smart, join the Hollywood famous and the

Hollywood rich and the Hollywood wise and the Hollywood wonderful. Just lift the best glassware ever fired, just sip the best Scotch ever aged, just look and listen, just tell them one and all how great they are, see what they think. They thought it was fascinating that this writer in person was actually not unlike everybody else at all of the Hollywood parties forever and forever.

About a year later an editor of a national magazine telephoned and said he had heard that I had met Jack Benny at a party and had told Jack Benny what his comedy really was, a kind of contemporary American folklore involving the vast astonishment of everybody about the crude and dishonest behavior of everybody else.

"We want to do a big important interview with Jack Benny," the man said, "but he told us to talk to you, so can you come in tomorrow to our office in Beverly Hills, so we can go to lunch and talk about this?"

By that time I lived in a house on the beach at Malibu, I was bankrupt, deep in debt, and needed money desperately.

I hung up and sat down and wrote a piece about Jack Benny, but also about myself of course, perhaps more about myself than about Jack Benny, and the next day went to lunch with the three editors at a very expensive restaurant.

After lunch the editor who had telephoned said, "Will you write a piece about Jack Benny for us? We'll pay our top fee, twenty-five hundred dollars."

I brought the folded manuscript out of my back pocket, and handed it to the man.

"Here it is," I said. "Just mail the check, please."

This scared the man half to death, but in the end the piece was published in *Look* precisely as I had written it.

James Agee, Konrad Bercovici, Jim Tully, and Charles Chaplin

EVERYBODY USED TO WRITE about Charles Chaplin. I knew him fairly well, spent time at his house in Beverly Hills, ate meals with him, heard him read from new scenarios, and so I *could* write about him, but I would rather try to remember some of the people he knew who remembered him fondly, like James Agee, who tried to help him with some of the dialogue in the autobiographical movie, *Limelight*, with its song which everybody in the world sang for so long, but which I cannot remember by melody or name, even now.

And I would like to try to remember some of the people who remembered Charles Chaplin with hatred and anger, like Jim Tully and Konrad Bercovici, each of whom had known him quite well, had done what I had done, listened to his scenarios and discussed them, and had actually worked with him on the scenarios, for which in the end they were not willingly paid any money at all, and either dropped the matter, as Jim Tully did, or took Charles Chaplin to court, as Konrad Bercovici did.

All the same, I liked him, even though he was quite plainly a kind of monster—genius has *got* to be, apparently. It seems to have to do with the sustained intensity of the determination to get something done.

A certain kind of genius has no choice. He comes out a monster, and that's the end of it.

For instance, I have a couple of recorded conversations in an office in Beverly Hills with my son in 1950 when he was seven, and with my daughter when she was not yet five.

A couple of years ago, coming upon the large disc on which these recordings were made, before the arrival of tape-recording machines, I decided to listen to them.

Doing so, I was abashed by the monster I had clearly been—loud, swift, impatient, unable to slow down, unable to be disciplined enough to make serene my nearness to each child, alone with me in an office. I *sounded* insensitive to them, and yet, this is the terrible and puzzling thing, I had been full of nothing but profound love, easy intelligence, abundant comedy, enormous health—and yet unmistakably a monster.

I could take it, about the boy, but when it came to the girl, I wept inside, and wished, great good God, how I wished that I could have done that half-hour with her quietly, slowly, softly, for God's sake, not as a stupid genius, not as a helpless roaring monster, but as a plain, simple, earnest, loving father.

I liked Charles Chaplin even *because he was* a monster, apart from his films, which are still the undisputed and undisputable triumph of the moving-picture business.

But even at that, even liking him, he was hard to take for longer than ten minutes, and that is the terrible thing about genius. You sometimes come upon such people who are not famous at all, who are unknown, but have that same damned monstrousness that comes out of excessive intensity of the self at odds with the hard environment or unyielding potential.

When such people have no fame, they are unbearable. Well, not to put too fine a point upon it, they are mad bores.

Oona O'Neill, very early in her marriage, took to going upstairs to privacy as soon as her husband began repeating his stories, his scenarios, his reminiscences, his identity, his legend, his tricks of communication, his pantomimes, his truth, his falsity, and it is to the everlasting glory of Charles Chaplin that he was not offended that his wife couldn't stand him at his best—or at his worst, or at any rate at his parlor performing of himself.

Konrad Bercovici had a huge moustache, he was short and stocky, and he wrote gypsy stories. He won his case, or Charles Chaplin's lawyer, Jerry Geisler, settled out of court, I forget which.

James Agee, with a lot of teeth removed from the front of his mouth, upper and lower, and without dental plates, gummed his brilliant talk to Charles Chaplin, and then back in New York one day, a passenger in a racing taxicab on his way to his psychiatrist, Agee suddenly had a fatal heart attack.

Jim Tully, about the same size as Konrad Bercovici but with very thick, very red hair, bore the burden of Charles Chaplin lightly. Tully's tragedy was his son, who was a compulsive rapist and consequently always in jail.

These are all geniuses, or monsters, as you prefer, and good men trying their best to make sense and to experience grace.

Trash along the Wabash,
Back Home in Indiana

I WENT TO PURDUE in 1960, flying from Paris to New York, and then to Chicago, in October or early November.

My work at Purdue was to end a little before Christmas, so that I could fly to San Francisco and put a fire in the fireplace of my study at 1821 15th Avenue and just sit there in the dark and look at the fire, as I had done the year the house had been built, 1939, sitting in a kind of ancient sobriety, if not stupor, listening to the whispering speech of the fire, and noticing the astonishing continuity of the upward flow of the flowers of flame, red, yellow, blue, green and white, large, small, in clusters, and in large and small explosions of form, action, and color. Just sit and think, and of course in 1939 part of what I thought was, "Here comes Armageddon, so where's my wife, and where are my children?"

In 1960 when I reached Purdue I had the answer all too full and final.

I thought, "Well, I'm here anyway, so I'll write a play just as I did six months ago in London, working out of a room at the Savoy Hotel, taking the underground every day to London's slums in the East End, to the theatre recently renamed Stratford East. And I will stage this Indiana play with the kids who are interested in acting at Purdue, just as I did in London."

And so it happened.

On Thanksgiving day my son and my daughter trained out from New York to Chicago, where I met them in a borrowed jalopy, and the next day drove them to my apartment on a hillside among trees in West Lafayette, so that we could have a little holiday together, a Thanksgiving feast in Chicago soon after their arrival, the jalopy drive to Purdue, and a long weekend thereafter.

They came to the rehearsals, the boy then seventeen, the girl fourteen.

I had gone up to Chicago in the rickety car the night before their arrival, which was scheduled to be around nine in the morning.

I had had an appointment with several people at *Playboy* and had run into the publisher himself, with his nose and his pipe. His brother took me around to see some of the establishment, one of his writers tagged along, a photographer took a lot of quick pictures in a kind of studio, and then I took a table at one of the rooms of the Club where a very good comic named Larry Storch was working. I began to drink dry martinis with the writer, who wanted to do an interview. He thought it might be useful to the interview he was doing, or was thinking of doing, if we were to go to a more traditional Chicago bar, too.

We went down to the street and hailed a taxi, but when the writer got out of the cab, he fell straight down onto the sidewalk. After he had been revived, I got him into another taxi, and he said he could get himself safely home. I had already had eight or nine martinis, but I went into the bar and had another martini, and then another, and then suddenly I was back in my room in the Pearson Hotel, looking through my wallet. It contained only two one-dollar bills instead of three or four twenties, and from one of the two inside card-holders, a one-hundred-dollar bill was gone.

Well, I had been rolled, that's all, and I didn't even know the name of the bar or its address, and the time was half-past three in the morning. I had been in Chicago about eight hours.

Forget it.

At seven I was up, shivering and sick, and then I was in a taxi going to Union Station, and the black man at the wheel was singing.

I sang with him: *Amazing grace, how sweet the sound, that saved a fool like me. I once was lost, but now am found, was blind, but now I see.*

Lear, Gogol, Napoleon, King Christian, and the Death of Ernest Hemingway

=================================

HAVE WE BEEN SILLY? Were we fools to try so hard? Did we sneak ourselves into the least and worst of the human dimensions of understanding and identity from the beginning? And can we never expect to get out and on into the largest and best?

Well, language is language, words are words, all we have is held fast in them, and we are stuck with language and our various usages of it.

Some languages don't have a word for certain things or ideas or realities. Not every language has a word for enemy, for instance. Of course, some languages have a dozen words for enemy, and one or two languages have three or four dozen words for that idea, and there is surely a language, possibly Latin, in which enemy and self are entwined into one word.

In any case, it isn't likely that anybody has reached the age of eight or nine without experiencing a sense of menace from himself, from his being, from his reality, from his mystery.

Have we been mistaken about ourselves? Especially in believing so earnestly that we ought to be something better, something like mortal royalty, or angelic commoners?

In trying to escape from our unwillingness to accept ourselves at any given moment, have we been silly? In killing ourselves, have we been an embarrassment? If so, to whom or to what? Which was the first language to hit upon the word for suicide?

Does the word mean anything? Did it come before the word for murder, or at the same time? Who does the suicide shoot when it seems that he has shot only himself? Who is put to sleep forever when the suicide takes a dozen pills when four are known to be deadly?

Well, of course, it is easy, and it is silly, to ask such questions, and easier and sillier to answer them, or to pretend to, but language is the house we inhabit, and words and sentences constitute the door, the hall, and the living room, and if the whole house is not what we thought it was, let it go, it will have to do until the whole thing settles down into a kind of spoken recitation in the form of a funny story, a joke, a parable, another order of meaninglessness, but this time at least amusing.

The telephone bell jangled one morning in Paris and somebody said, "This is Raoul Tannenbaum at *Time* magazine, and we would like to know your reaction to the news that Ernest Hemingway this morning shot himself and is dead. Would you write something out for us?"

I wrote something, saying I considered the shot an accident.

It wasn't that he hadn't done the thing deliberately and with a certain amount of ingeniousness, it was simply that it was an accident that he had found it unavoidable to be deliberate and ingenious in that manner, that's all.

But *Time* didn't run what they had *asked* me to send them, free of charge. And why did I send them *anything?* What did I know about Ernest Hemingway? What did I know about suicide?

I was shocked. I was sorry, not only because Ernest Hemingway was dead, but because I myself was in a fight that could suddenly become deadly. I was broke. I was in debt. My career as a writer was shot. I was fighting the world. I hated publishers, editors, agents, critics, book reviewers, newspapers, magazines, publicity agents, lawyers, dentists, and taxi drivers. I owed the Tax Collector so much money there just didn't seem to be any way I could possibly both pay him off and keep myself alive—and now Ernest Hemingway was dead. It had to be an accident, pure and simple.

And I hated that kind of accident.

Well, again we're stuck, being who we are, what we are, the trivial enormity that we are, there just isn't any alternative, and there never has been—the best we can hope for is Lear by way of Shakespeare, the Russian petty clerk of Gogol's *The Overcoat,* Napoleon in the snow suddenly the laughingstock of the world, hearing its derisive laughter in his *own* disbelieving, almost silent, almost sobbing laughter, and Sibelius inconsolable in *The King Christian Suite*—each of them part of the whole mortal error, absurdity, and desperate grandeur that holds us all together.

The Joy of Aram's Soul,
the Pride of Araxie's Heart

THEY BROUGHT him as an infant to the frame house at 2226 San Benito Avenue in Fresno, and left him, so that they could go to a wedding, and then to a reception and a party that was going to go on all night: his handsome young father Aram and his beautiful young mother Araxie. He was their firstborn, and the joy of Aram's soul, and the pride of Araxie's heart.

The minute they were out of the house, though, he began to cry, and he cried all night.

I heard every minute of his crying, and I tried to understand it, for it seemed to demand that it be understood: it was not an infant's crying.

The crying made me believe that centuries of human anguish had been born into this one little soul, and that it was this awful anguish that was making the infant cry.

Are we sure that Jesus as an infant did not weep for the human race in that same manner? Or is the trick to postpone the tears until you're thirty years old? Or what?

In any event, as the infant wept I thought about all of us and how always near to despair we really are, except for something else equally powerful in us, a kind of balance to the despair, a sense of life as a blindly joyous action, a totally unreasonable, unjustified and unjustifiable sense that the reality of *being* is the most desirable of alternatives.

Imagine, for instance, not quite being. Out of the billions of chances involved, imagine not quite making it. And then suddenly after perhaps another billion years, imagine having the *right* two elements clash and embrace, and put us out into the light to be human beings. And then imagine the simple comedy of this long-postponed and finally meaningless but very useful and precious accident of *being*— instead of eons more of not being. Well, we might as well *be*. So what's the crying for?

God Almighty, I'm me at last, and I love me, although I seem to hate the rest of the human race, and if the strictest truth is told I also really hate myself, and yet somehow I love myself, as if I were God, or the whole thing, all of it unreasonable, and so contradictory as to be not worth bringing up to full thought and rejection, letting it stay just below the level of reality itself, but deeply felt just the same, lightly, swiftly, and always with a certain sense of absurdity.

Is everybody born into the world to die for the sins of the human race?

In infancy, does *everybody* weep for the whole human race?

Well, *that* infant certainly did, and I heard him, and it troubled me, and it hasn't stopped troubling me, although at this late date, whatever the truth about his weeping may be, I am equal to it, and cannot be surprised, disappointed, let down, amazed, or made to feel that I have been an awful fool for more than half a century for believing there was more to it than what is taken for granted by everybody sensible since the beginning of time: he is crying for himself, for no reason at all, but because infants cry, that's all.

Well, is that so? Do they cry for no reason at all?

As a small boy I asked my mother a number of times about my own nature and identity as an infant.

"You could be left with the old Portuguese woman who lived next door," she said, "and you were perfectly happy."

This pleased me, and made me feel that I was another of the chosen souls of the world, although it is probably more likely that the truly chosen soul doesn't linger too long, for having *been* chosen.

Well, finally this fellow, my favorite cousin, by name Guytzak, or Spark, doused himself with gasoline, drove his little blue car along a country road at Piedra, deliberately guided the car over a twenty-foot embankment, lighted a match, heard the explosion, felt the bang of the car upon the abandoned railroad spur of the Southern Pacific, leaped out of his shoes by reflex, breathed fire and smoke, collapsed, and lingered for twelve hours in the Army Hospital in Fresno, being fed plasma, and asking, "I'm not going to die, am I?"

He was a rare one. He cried that whole night as an infant.

Willie Willie Whiskey Everlasting Saroyan, Friend of Fools

════════════════════════════════

WHAT A FOOL I've been all my life, and how right it has been for me, what a blessing in disguise, as the saying is, always unable not to defy the odds. Unable not to insist that God is on my side, mystery is with me, in the making of proper choices. Even if I make the wrong choice, something metaphysical will make it the right choice, and again I will win, I will be the winner, there will be a perfect demonstration of the righteousness of being a good man, a perfect demonstration of the intelligence of being decent, the practicality of hating nobody, the superiority of not being afraid of anybody or anything, of being everybody's best acquaintance—not friend, that would be a little fatheaded and presumptuous. Everybody's best acquaintance: "You are not going to lose, Sir, because I am here, and you will be just fine. I have looked at you and seen beyond your ugliness a child of luminous beauty, you are going to find yourself, Sir, your amnesia is going to come to a joyous end, you are going to say in a soft voice, 'By God I am me, after all, and it is painless for me to be myself, and I don't have to have any more amnesia.'"

I never elected to be a fool, it just came to me. And the folly had enough intelligence in it to permit me to put up with all of the mystery and meaninglessness.

If I weren't a fool, if I hadn't always been a fool, would

I, to begin with, compel people everywhere to smile immediately upon my arrival among them, as I had done at the Fred Finch Orphanage, not yet three?

Why did they smile?

And when I spoke, why did they break into laughter?

And to this day in front of an audience, if I happen to flick the end of my nose with a finger to drive away the tickling there, why does the whole audience break into loud laughter and applause, as if I had just said something amusing or had done something that did indeed mean something?

If I wasn't a fool, would I *know* that my work is writing, for the reason that at the age of nine I discovered that books are not like trees and animals, productions of nature and God, but are written by men? Thinking, if any man can do something with words, then of course I can, too, can't I? Especially since my handwriting is art, is calligraphy, is impossible *not* to see and read and understand. And aren't the words I write words of courteous concern for the reader, whoever he may be, don't the words reveal a member of the only royal family the human race has ever known, with a halo around his head if you don't happen to be blind, and the light of the ages in his eyes beholding everything with admiration and gratitude, and everybody with delight and love.

Oh boy, what a fool. Look at him go. Even now, well along into his sixty-eighth year, look at the mortal son of the immortal mother go.